D1549646

ENGINE-DRIVING LIFE.

ENGINE-DRIVING LIFE.

Stirring Adventures and Incidents
IN THE LIVES OF LOCOMOTIVE ENGINE-DRIVERS

BY

MICHAEL REYNOLDS.

EDITED AND PRESENTED BY MAURICE RICKARDS.

London

HUGH EVELYN.

THIS EDITION FIRST PUBLISHED IN 1968 BY
HUGH EVELYN LTD., 9 FITZROY SQUARE, LONDON W.1.
THIS EDITION © 1968, MAURICE RICKARDS.
S.B.N. 238.78908.X.
PRINTED AND BOUND IN THE REPUBLIC OF IRELAND BY
HELY THOM LIMITED.

CONTENTS.

CHAPTER I.

INTRODUCTION.

THE locomotive engine is the most beautiful mechanical construction of this or any other time. We watch it under steam from a distance, from meadows where in the sun the cattle graze, and it seems to fly as the swallows fly—skimming above the horizon, and presently we see its colossal form crossing the mighty arches which span the valley of the river. Then we on the platform shrink from it aghast as it rushes past in the full thunder of its power, and, straining on its course like some mighty monster broken loose, it is an object of intense and almost passionate interest. Hence it is that volunteers are never wanting among us for the wild-like life of the rail.

There are many facts in our railway life that pass unnoticed and unrecorded, and are lost in oblivion; for few there are who witness the struggle for advancement, who search for the platines of fine gold and bring them to the surface.

The battle of life absorbs all our energies, and it is because we are not all cast in the same mould that now and again we hear of adventures which throw fresh light on the history of men, their character and deeds, and the record of which enables others to trace the reflection of their own experience.

Reticence on the part of engine-men has always prevailed; and it is easily accounted for in the fact that few have at any time been of the same opinion on any locomotive question: even the acutest have at times been wrong. I remember a good engine-man complaining about his engine not being able to run at high speed, saying that she was wrapped up, meaning that she had too much lap on the valve, whereas there was nothing of the kind; the cause of her failing to attain a high speed was that the steam-ports were too small to admit the steam in and out of the cylinder with sufficient freedom to admit of a quick speed of piston.

The practice of locomotive driving is a field teeming with facts and incidents, cause and effect leading up by natural and consistent steps towards perfection through long winter nights in wind and in rain, in lightning and thunder; at all times surrounded by hidden dangers, and ending at times in a dreadful, sudden death. A man may have the best of locomotive knowledge, and still, if he is unaware how and where others have met with accidents, he will be assaulted by surprises, and his progress will be but slow.

Distinctly predominant among the causes of surprise is the uncertain nature of the materials by means of which he earns his bread. Uncertain is the material over which his engine glides, and fallible are the men amongst whom he works and on whom his life as a driver depends, as the swift wheel turns round and round. Everything about him is in action, at war one with another—wear and tear, time and decay.

How much real public service is done by cautioning men where others have failed, we never can know. We, however, must snatch a few lessons of experience from oblivion.

CHAPTER II.

THE ENGINE-FIREMAN—FORMATION OF CHARACTER.

"A ROLLING stone gathers no moss." So says the proverb, and it is true. Activity is not sufficient to insure success unless it be directed to one invariable end. The path that leads to success must be pursued through all its asperities and obliquities—that is, if we wish to reach the object in view. The traveller who turns aside to gather every flower, or who hurries and sometimes loiters, will soon find that he is being left behind in the race to reach the goal. If we deviate from the track, our competitors go by, and it is then no easy matter to recover the lost ground. Onwards and upwards in earnest is the only way to attain a higher level.

There are aspirants for the foot-plate in whose natures there is something that revolts against the practical; who soar for a time with an imposing aspect, looking high and reaching out far, but they fail to sustain themselves on the wing, and they imperceptibly drop out of sight amongst the crowd. They started with views unique in presumption and utterly irreconcilable with common sense, and after they have been in the steam-shed a few months and become just nicely acquainted with oil, waste, fire-carrying, and night-work, they suddenly wake up and find the prize of their ambition lies further afield than they expected, through years of patient toil, and they begin to think there is no more chance of reaching the object they set out for than the man in the moon. For a time they run well, but lacking the force of perseverance they become utterly bewildered by the ascending ground they have to encounter.

The steps of a locomotive engine leading on to the foot plate land the engine-cleaner on the first landing in his aspiring labour, from which he can look back upon the way he has come, and reflect upon the clamour, the struggle, the unrest which make up the world about him.

To reach the foot-plate as a passed fireman is an accomplishment that thousands have tried at and failed—failed through indolence, through fatigue to pursue, failed through loss of hope and interest, failed because the flower appeared above the beds ready to be grasped. To those who have so far surmounted the difficulties we would say, Let the success which has attended you in the ascent stimulate you to energetic aspirations, and rest not until the topmost round of that Jacob's ladder of progress is reached.

Upon the foot-plate there are, at first, many things to attract a fireman's attention and thoughts. With change of scene, in the presence of objects brighter and more congenial than torchlight, cans of cleaning oil, bath-brick, and waste, the pulse is quickened; he regains his health and spirits as the links which bind him to those objects are broken one by one, and as his sympathies are drawn to the things immediately about him.

A fireman was once found almost beside himself sweeping

up and wiping down the foot-plate. "What is the matter, my fellow?" asked the foreman. "I am happy now, sir," answered the man. When that is so, no matter in what sphere it is, there is a clear sky overhead, and the sun shines on the life which sails on a springtide of hope and gratitude, in proud consciousness of having achieved a triumph. With an overflow of spirits, which in its prodigal excess counts no toil and fears no exhaustion, a fireman begins his career with very little knowledge of the locomotive, excepting the names of its various parts. He has the key to the locomotive to unlock all its boxed-up treasures, but all his stock of information bundled together would not detect a screw loose in the lock, or give the clue to such symptoms as bring engines to grief.

The driver is in charge of the engine, and it is his place to give the fireman a completer knowledge of his duties, and if he has faults he should see that every day mends one. It is a lesson to show him how to handle the shovel, how to shoot the coals off it as clean as shot into the fire-box, into the very place intended for them to lie. It is a lesson to show him how to prepare the engine, so that he can pack both glands, after he has been taught that the packing is a trimming as much as any other about the engine. It is a lesson to teach him how to take the bulk of the momentum out of the train with the brake, and then to slower the train under control to the platform. It is a lesson to teach him that many others have choked fires and stopped trains by making the fire too deep for the load. It is a lesson to tell him that it is possible to be a fireman without being as black as a tinker. It is a lesson to teach him that on an engine there should be a place for everything, and everything in its place. Where common sense prevails on the foot-plate, and the driver is well ballasted and moves on an even keel, and is not carried away by the winds of passion or warped by prejudice, and is not quick to heed the sanguine temperament of a young fireman, all is well. We must all learn, he knows. On the other hand, a fireman who gets on is circumspect; that is, as the etymology of the word indicates, he looks all round before venturing to act independently of the driver.

Firemen are, at the outset, appointed with drivers in charge of shunting-engines; that is, a class of engines designed generally without tenders, as they carry the supply of coal and water upon the engine-frame. Such engines are generally termed tank-engines. By means of them, the goods waggons, as they leave the loading shed, are arranged and formed into trains. That is, they put, say in Camden yard, all the waggons for Liverpool on one road; all those for Manchester on another; and the Scotch goods on a third road, and so on, ready for the engine to take them to their destination right through. Such trains are called express goods.

On the shunting-engine the young fireman learns to handle the brake, so as to bring the engine up to the waggons without

loss of time, and without damaging them. He learns also, in a limited way, how to handle the shovel; how to put an injector "on" and "off;" and he acquires a bit of knowledge respecting coupling up. As he cannot move about the yard without signals, he finds that *green* signifies caution, or come up steady; *red* to indicate danger, and stop; and *white*, "all right." He has to hold points occasionally, and at the first pair he takes hold of, he trembles from head to foot for fear the engine should take a dislike to him and jump off the road. He then runs after the engine, and at first follows and jumps upon the hinder buffer-plank, so that if he does not succeed, and falls down, the engine runs away from him, instead of running over him. He grows bolder, and thinks no more of turning an engine through a double set of points, and following it up by jumping on to the step whilst the engine is moving, than of eating his supper. He makes friends, and chats with the chaps in the shunters' cabin, and enjoys it mightily, for he is in the midst of railway talk, surrounded by men who have a strange history of their own. In such company, the young fireman hears the story of a smash that made the hills rattle, and piled the waggons up into the air; and how Tom Hassock was found under the débris, alive and well, inside an empty sugar-cask. Jim Jeffery, a short, thick-set man, with coarse features, two or three warts on his face, and one eye nearly closed, relates a story how he made half-a-dozen men jump nearly out of their hides, who were taking their breakfast inside a box-waggon in a goods warehouse with closed doors. He had three waggons to leave at the place, which was situated at the bottom of an incline. The waggons were detached from the train at the top, and slowed down the incline by the guard, who rode upon one of the waggons so as to control the brake. The incline was a long one, and Jeffery, who had been down many a time before with waggons, knew the maximum speed to allow before beginning to slow. Placing his foot upon the brake-lever, he pressed the brake-block against the wheel with the whole of his weight; and had scarcely reduced the speed when the block slewed off the face of the wheel, and Jeffery was on his back in an instant on the road. The trucks ran away without anything to impede them, until they drove right into the shed-door at the south end, knocking the box-waggon and men out through the north door, up against the scotch-blocks outside, and were only prevented from following by the outraged wooden structure falling bodily into the top of them. Jim Jeffery was a great treat with his quaint looks, and story-telling attractions; and, when he once began his stream of anecdotes, they flowed like oil from a barrel. Such are the kind of peeps a young hand gets of the troubles that railway men have to contend with.

After a fireman has been engaged in forming trains, and has learned to distinguish signals, and to ply the shovel pretty freely, he is promoted to the platform of a goods-engine—the pick-up goods—running from station to station, setting "off" and picking "up" waggons; leaving a crate of fowl at Four Ashes, a flitch of bacon at Spread Eagle, and a barrel of flour at Penkridge. These are called box goods; and by shunting at different places for the passenger trains and express goods, he learns the position of signals, the road, and the traffic. It is this kind of knowledge which a man requires in order to work locomotive engines without over-shooting the signals, or the stations, or delaying passenger trains. However well a mechanic may understand the mechanism of an engine, he would be completely lost with one under steam on a strange road.

With slow goods-trains, any little heating, or heavy firing, can be rectified without causing any delay; and that such things do happen with young drivers and young firemen is well known. They are both under training; the former to feel his position as a driver, and the latter to learn how to work so that at all times he may be able to perform his duties *in the right way,* and no other.

On slow goods-trains the fireman is permitted to do a little oiling; that is, to handle the oil-can, and fill up some of the syphons on the road, and tallow the swabs suspended on the piston-rod, and valve-spindle studs. Beyond filling up on the road, he is not allowed more oiling by shrewd drivers, who like to oil the engine themselves before leaving the shed, so that they can see if all the trimmings are in the syphons and boxes; for "ratting" goes on about a railway as well as in factories; he can also see if the trimmings are working and passing the oil.

Some drivers who have had hot big-ends or hot slide-bars, and been obliged to give up their trains, have rather prized the opportunity of showing the foreman that the syphon was actually full of oil at the time of the accident, and that therefore there could not be any negligence. But the proof of so much oil was a proof of negligence, and showed that the trim-

EXTERIOR OF THE SIGNAL BOX AT A LONDON RAILWAY TERMINUS.

ming had become old and worthless, being no better than a cork, and would not work. From oiling he is allowed to advance a step further, and take the management of the fire into his own hands, and feed the boiler with water. With slow trains, the fireman obtains a further insight into the dangers attending locomotive life; such, for instance, as being knocked off the tender by bridges which span the railway, or by columns which support them, or by going underneath an engine in a siding without seeing that the tender-brake is hard on. He also comes in contact with disabled engines with broken crank-shafts, broken excentric-rods, excentric-straps and sheaves, broken motion, and broken springs; and he obtains an opportunity of seeing how, under such circumstances, engines are temporarily repaired to get them home. Above all, which is the most important, he hears, if he does not actually see, what has been the cause of such failures; and he is therefore, so far as possible, cautioned against running into the same dangers. If the question were asked, Do firemen break engines down? we could state many facts to prove that they do. It may be both interesting and useful to mention a few instances, like caution-boards stuck up by the side of a wood, intimating that "man-traps" are concealed under the leaves and ferns.

Foremost appears on the list the bugbear, a choked fire, which in thousands of cases has upset the working of all classes of trains from slow goods to fast expresses—especially so a few years ago, before any system of firing was introduced. Firemen have neglected raking out the ash-pan, and thereby brought down the fire-bars and the fire into the ash-pan; they have neglected to protect the bars before making up a fire; they have neglected to fill the tender at a water-crane—taking a splash of water to indicate that the tender was completely filled; they have neglected to fill the sand-box, and the engine has in consequence slipped and slipped until a crank-pin has broken; they have been intrusted with the oiling too soon, and not knowing how much oil such and such bearing should take, they have been satisfied with the performance of filling the cups to the brim, and at the same time provident and

cautious not to waste any oil, and not for a moment suspecting their own want of experience in oiling. There is not the skilful keenness of perception requisite to detect deviations, and indeed his mind can only be trained by the hard-earned experience of disappointment. A big-end or an excentric starts cutting its bearing after he has oiled it, and suspicion falls upon him. It may happen that the engine is effectually disabled, and in the face of a heated bearing, what proof has he to show that he performed his work honestly and thoroughly, for the heat has burned out the trimming, and the oil has fumed away? When there is no apparent possibility of a proof for good or for evil being obtained, flesh and blood become weary, and the effect is unpleasant. The driver and his fireman are apt under such circumstances to indulge in weak complimentary language, and the skin of each becomes so thin on such occasions, by sputter and retorts, that it is ready to give out. After a failure or two of this kind, a fireman begins to be weary of himself; but the railway people know that he must learn for himself in the morning of life, and he goes brooding upon his small stock of material, counting upon results oddly enough delusive. How a fireman may obtain information, how far his surroundings must be his teachers, how much he will owe to inspection, and how much to the kindness of his drivers, it is difficult to say; but we know this, if a fireman is to become a workman that "needeth not to be ashamed," he must not be disappointed if some one tells him that in locomotive engines and locomotive working there is sufficient material to fill some scores of books, and that the only way to make it one's own is to go into the work with a will, and steadily follow it up.

From firing on goods-engines, where he is supposed to have learned all about firing, all about oiling, all about signals, a fireman in time climbs, by order of his foreman, on to a passenger engine; and it would be idle to try and prove how welcome this promotion is after from three to five years on the goods-engines. The hours on duty are much reduced now, compared with what they were. But eighteen or twenty hours a day on duty have been a very common occurrence, on an engine without any weather-board, and with wet sand-boxes, and in all sorts of hard weather, and we suspect in some instances with hard fare—very hard; but they have been buoyed up with the thought that their passenger days were ahead.

Very few firemen give up the pursuit, for the simple reason that many of them, with a pause in their shovelling, have thrown a kiss to a milkmaid, and wedlock has been the result, with eighteen shillings a week and overtime. And many couples dwell together as a pair of roses. There may be weary trips in cold weather, and danger; but there is ease of mind, and the humble meal is eaten with much love, and what the dinner basket does not contain the heart does not crave after. But, mingled with affection, the young wife soon learns the dangers to which the persevering husband is exposed—the toil, the struggle, the hairbreadth escapes. She feels the heart-ordeal that may be hers after her neighbour's is over; such thoughts eclipse half the sunshine of her home and life. But that young heart is strong in faith, assured that there is no limit to answered prayers. In the year's roll of accidents to railway servants we find that, taking averages, a fireman is killed every fortnight, and two permanently injured every week, while performing their duties. It would be well, with the hope of saving some, to note how, when, and where some firemen have been suddenly overtaken by the hand of death.

It is impossible to disguise the fact that many firemen lose their lives through the drivers moving the engine while the firemen are underneath, owing to the latter having gone there without mentioning it to the driver. Several very painful instances have occurred in which a brother has killed a brother, a father a son. Now, in most cases of accidents by the machinery of the engine, a most important duty has been neglected— the sounding of the whistle before moving the engine has been omitted to be done. In the instance of the brother fatally injuring his brother, the poor young fellow was underneath the boiler oiling the big-ends, and his brother was asked by the station-master to make some shunts for him, when he, as smart a driver as ever stood upon a foot-plate, jumped on to the foot-

plate and put on steam. It was entirely through his desire to act promptly that caused him to move without whistling.

Not a few men have run to the back of a tender for a fire-iron, or for something out of the tool-box, and been struck by a bridge and killed on the spot. The writer was once struck down by one, but miraculously escaped being killed, through the engine happening to be going tender first. Several express firemen and drivers have been killed through leaning over the engine too far, so that they came in contact with some pillars supporting a bridge or the covering of a platform; and some very smart, promising young men have been killed when oiling, through not maintaining their hand-hold. One was letting tallow into the cylinders in front, and the engine at the time was just coming over the top of a bank, and the waggons gave a sudden snatch, owing to the steam having been shut off too soon, which gave the engine a sharp check, and he fell over the buffer-beam in front and under the engine. Another was oiling the motion from the framing, and when the engine entered through a pair of points in a sharp curve, causing it to give a lurch, he fell off and was run over by the whole of the train, and was quite dead when he was taken up. There is no doubt that many such accidents could be prevented if the men would not be so self-confident; and, what is more to be deplored, these accidents, which bring sorrow and sore affliction, do frequently occur to the best of the men, whose judgment one would be inclined to think would make them wary of danger. But there is no doubt that living, moving, and breathing in an atmosphere of danger daily does harden the nerves, and tend to make men careless, and to furnish their minds with a notion that they are exempt from suffering, or from a dreadful death. On passenger-trains a fireman has to perform pretty nearly the same duties as he did upon the goods-trains, but with some important distinctions. The generation of the steam is the same, the coal is the same; in many cases—in fact, in most cases— the boilers are the same, only they supply steam to move round a larger wheel at a higher speed. But, on the passenger-trains, the fireman has to take charge of the fire and feed, he makes up his own fire, he manages it himself, he fires when it is necessary, he knows the difference between good and bad firing, between good and bad coal, and how to get along with small and large coal; he keeps the steam up, and the boiler safe with water, for hundreds of miles in the course of a week without any instructions being asked for, or thought necessary to be given by the driver, who has his own duties to perform in attending to his engine, in listening to the beats, in seeing the signal all right, in observing the movements of the passing traffic, and following out the instructions of the weekly and daily notices.

The duties the fireman has to perform on express engines may have been partially learned, or completely learned, long before he left the goods-engine. But, on the express engines, he has to accelerate the speed of his movements, to economise his time by thinking beforehand, and to get through his work without hurrying—without making unnecessary work. He must mark right in the centre, if you will, and make "bull's-eyes" every time. To work as a fireman on an express, he must, to give satisfaction, have studied separately every question connected with the working of the engine; he must have questioned the reason of all things until the marvel became only a portion of his knowledge. From the fact of engines failing through choked fires, he finds there is a law which governs combustion. It is no longer a mystery; he can divine the cause. Too much on? he can expound the reason. Too little blast or air? he can predict the result—shortness of steam. From the fact of a box heating, he can reason in the same way and apply the remedy. So then, in his experience chance has no existence; and coming upon duty, and while on duty, and when off duty, he knows that for similar effects there are constant causes; and to avoid accidents and failures, to which firemen can contribute, he must remove the cause, and see that it is kept at a distance. In the performance of his duties, he has much to think about, as steam must be made as fast as it is required. Every shovelful of coal must find its proper billet, and the shovel on fast expresses must move between fire-door and coal as though it were too hot to hold.

That foot-plate is the most free from disorder, most replete with purpose, on which intelligence is to be seen in every act. There, there is power to fathom all things pertaining to locomotive work and railway running.

CHAPTER III.

THE ENGINE-DRIVER—HIS PROGRESS.

On the foot-plate we see only, in the position of driver, a man who has reached the regulator through many vicissitudes, break-downs, collisions, explosions, dreadfully cold nights, and still more dreadful dangers, always moving amidst a ceaseless change of things, himself unchanged. If we were to sum up the conditions on which a man can command the regulator of an engine, it would read thus:—Miles to run, 200,000; coals to break up and put into the fire-box in their proper place, 3,000 tons; day work, 3 years; night work, 4 years; Sunday work, 25 days per year; innumerable hairbreadth escapes, eyes constantly on the roll, the mouth shut and the ears open, an iron constitution, a whistle in the lips, a warm heart, and an intelligent head, with the motto, "Wait."

We see, then, on the foot-plate men who have been well drilled for the work, who can pride themselves upon having one qualification if no other—loyal servitude. Before they obtain charge, they have, as a matter of course, been scrutinised by those who have the welfare of the service at heart, and who are desirous of bringing to the front such men as will tend to give satisfaction to the directors of the railway and to the public.

The localities where such men are to be looked for are the foot-plates of the express engines; they are there simply by merit, by having achieved results.

Some work their way more rapidly than others—come to perfection sooner—looking like promising fellows in the gait, in the look, and the tact with which they go about their work. If a man works his mind as well as his shovel, it gives to tne character a manly bearing. He faces difficulties and disappointments with no obliquity in the vision, with singleness of eye, and a oneness of purpose, in the midst of boundless trivialities so called.

From better to better. Every-day things must be done better and smarter to-day than they were done a month back.

Work upon the inner man and it will tell upon the outer man. It will not suffice to limit ourselves to the bare acquisition of such knowledge as is absolutely necessary for present purposes, we must stretch out on this side and on that, cherishing and making much of whatever we find within us. We must let nothing slip, but confront every locomotive and railway question coming within our sphere with a determination to shake the truth out of it at any price, and proceeding on to the next puzzle, working heartily and thoroughly in a manly spirit, rising slowly and surely to perfection, if perfection there be.

They are not all models on the express engines, either in appearance or for picking up the irregularities of foot-plate life and throwing them overboard. To some men everything is proper. Nothing looks more reasonable than to expect that a young driver who has been brought up on the foot-plate with a first-class driver should start well, continue, and end well;

but in scores of instances they have ignominiously failed as drivers, by committing all the blunders that locomotive driving is liable to. We shall have no difficulty in tracing the cause of this. All of us more or less ignore the teaching of facts, as facts are in relation to other folks and not to ourselves. Every locomotive superintendent knows that scores of engines have been disabled through the drivers attempting to leave a siding before the points were open, when, consequently, the engine was "trapped." There is not a line in the country without traps of this kind; and there is not a driver on these lines but also has either seen or heard of their comrades having their engines de-railed in them; and yet, the drivers knowing this, there is an engine off in these traps on some lines every week.

The science of locomotive-driving is based upon experience and observation.

Things appertaining to the foot-plate find their place in men's experience, and but little in books; and so it is on the foot-plate that we must now proceed to take a glimpse of a race of men, or a class of men, who do good service for their country. When a fireman is passed for a driver, the promotion is, as a rule, in his own mind, twelve months or two years behind time. But a man is generally about five years before he is capable of taking the responsibility of a driver upon his shoulders. Of course, railway companies recognise the great principle of individual exertion; they make every man in the service stand *alone* upon his merits, and strictly accountable for the rapidity of his own promotion. It is the principle that appeals to that Anglo-Saxon energy which performs its own part without looking round to see what others are doing. The space and facilities are grand for every man to raise himself to the perfection of an employé on the locomotive; but the pyramid of his attainment, as already referred to, must be of his own designing and building. With all the advantages of working and travelling, seeing and hearing, if a fireman cares not to raise himself above animal servitude, he will always have a deal of mud and slush about him to discomfort him, and his level will be that of trite humanity.

But if he erects for himself a high standard of excellence and despises mediocrity, he will soon find himself raised from the fluid shifting mass some feet, and sufficiently high to look *down* and into every question connected with railway working. Let there be no misunderstanding; promotion depends, like reaping, upon sowing. The farmer sacrifices a certain portion of his corn in order to gain a harvest; a fireman must sacrifice a portion of his attention in order to qualify himself for his business as a driver by gathering a mass of miscellaneous information, arranging and labelling it, ready for use. The railway locomotive superintendents need men for their engines just as much as men need engines, and those firemen who are distinguished for their fulness of knowledge of the engine and the exigencies of the service are selected.

Drivers are drivers; their engines are selected for them, like their positions, by the foreman, who has under him a staff of men and sub-foremen to prepare the engines for the road, and to have them in steam for the drivers to work. It may interest some persons to follow more in detail this process of preparation, as everything in connection with locomotives is becoming more and more particularly interesting to the public.

*   *   *   *   *

In the running-shed there are gangs of men told off for certain work, and no other, with a foreman over them. There are the fitters, who do all repairs—temporary repairs; there are the coal-men, who coal the engines; there are the washer-outs, who wash the boilers *inside*; there are the cleaners, who clean the boiler outside; there is the turner with his men to light up, and raise steam by the time the driver is booked on duty.

When the driver went " off " duty, he told the coal-men how much coal to put on the tender, and what kind of coal, if there were several kinds at the coal-stage; and if Welsh coal was amongst them he would be sure to ask for some, whether he got any for asking or not. If the supply was rather limited, and the driver one of those straightforward men who never " tip," the chances are he would get none. The ganger of coal-men writes down in a book the amount of coal he delivers to each engine, and this is compared with the number of miles run by the engine, and the weight of coal consumed by each engine in a month, divided by the miles run, gives the weight of coal in pounds consumed per mile, and by this means the superintendent finds out *the man* who is the heaviest in fuel, and *the man* who is the lightest in fuel.

A monthly sheet is made out and posted up in the running-shed, setting forth the various shades of good and bad engine-manship, by informing all and sundry how much coal each man

has burned per mile. It is fair work to get on and keep time with Welsh coal at 25 lbs. per mile; with Derbyshire coal at 28 lbs. per mile. A standard is fixed by which the men's work is estimated. On some lines the drivers are allowed 14 lbs. of coal per mile per engine, 1½ lbs. of coal per mile for a carriage, and 1¼ lbs. of coal per mile for a waggon. So that if a driver made a run of fifty miles with eighteen carriages, on the above standard scale, he would be allowed in total, for engine and carriages, 2,050 lbs., or 18¼ cwt. of coal; and if he performed the journey with 12¼ cwt., he would obtain sixpence, or one penny per cwt.

Coal premiums have been much abused, and by good drivers

they are thought very little of as a measure of ability. It has been found out that the outlay of threepence in a pint of ale would, in some cases, land 6 cwt. of coal on a tender, and the coal-man would never see it; and the next tender that came would receive 6 cwt. with the tender feeling the weight of it, and still the coal-man saw it put on.

Then, again, a driver and a guard managed to do a little quiet business together, and at the end of the month squared up. The guard holds a ticket belonging to the driver, on which he enters the time of departure from one station and the arrival-time at another, together with the number of trucks attached to the engine, in order to show how much coal the driver should consume in hauling them between stations.

The guard booked fifty waggons, when there were only thirty, so that the driver would obtain credit for twenty times 1¼ lbs. of coal per mile for waggons which he never saw.

This work went on for some time, until the bubble burst, and then all the coal premium that enginemen—there were several in this predicament—had taken in their lives—in some instances £20—they had to pay back in weekly instalments of 5s. each, and forfeit all their share in premiums for the future. This was stiff punishment, and still not too severe, in order to produce a good effect throughout the whole body of engine-men.

After an engine is coaled, it is taken into the shed and cleaned inside by the washers twice a week, and outside every night or every day by the cleaner. About three hours before the engine is required, the bar-boy comes along with a torch-lamp, steel broom, and fire-bar lifter, and enters the fire-box to clean it of clinkers, to sweep down the tube-plate, and to re-arrange the bars. After him follows the fire-lighter with a short shovel and hammer: he breaks a few lumps of coal up on half-a-dozen engines, and then goes to the furnace, where about a ton of coal is all on a blaze, and shouts out " Fire, fire." The foreman cleaner hears this, and dispatches half-a-dozen youths to carry fire in long shovels on their shoulders to the engines. This done they go to their cleaning again. The fire-lighter adds fresh coal to that which is now just put into the fire-box—about 1½ cwt.—and after he has assured himself that it is lighted, he, in his rounds, looks in on it occasionally, and takes stock of what steam the engine is making. If an engine is too forward, he lowers the damper, and if another is too slow, he exerts himself to forward the fire, either by putting wood on or getting the engine under the " blower "—a contrivance that has cracked many a boiler. It consists of a piece of tubing (¾ inch), having one end in the chimney of an engine and the other attached to a boiler containing steam, which is allowed to escape by means of a cock through a pipe. As the steam issues from the orifice of the pipe, it induces a current of air to ascend through the fire, the tubes, and the chimney—in fact, it blows up the fire. The same effect, though in a different manner, is produced by running an engine about in reversed gear by means of another engine.

Following the fire-lighter is the shed-turner, who is responsible for the engines being in steam; he now and again pays each engine a visit, and casts his eye at the steam-gauge. More than once, since railways started, the turner has looked and looked for steam in vain, and then found the boiler red-hot, having been lighted up without water in it. Such cases are rare, but when they do happen there is the " sack " for the fire-lighter, a fine for the turner, and the postponement of an increase of salary for the foreman. Again, there is the fitter; he contrives, if possible, to do all the little repairs required before the time is due to leave the shed.

All the repairs which the drivers think are necessary, to work their engines and trains with punctuality, are entered in a book kept for the purpose, in charge of the foreman fitter, who writes down opposite each case the name of the fitter he has chosen to do such and such work. Amongst his men he finds those who can let a big-end together better than others, and nearly every one has an aptitude for some special work, on which he is mostly employed. One man is noted for making joints, another for lifting and putting in a brass, another for valve-setting, while some are of no note or likelihood.

When the driver arrives, his engine is ready for him—coaled, cleaned, repaired, and in steam; and he takes possession at once, about an hour before train-time. The engine-men are in what are called " links; " that is, groups of from eight to a dozen, as may be required, to work the expresses. Then follow second express-men; then men for fast passenger-trains, which make several intermediate stops at stations, past which the above " fly " by; then men for slow passenger-trains; then men for slow-trains. On the goods-trains the like order pre-

LEEDS STATION FROM HOLBECK JUNCTION.

vails—express, slow or pick-up-goods, and short trains. There is an auxiliary "link," consisting of engine-men who are ready with engines to go and do anything—"banking," "piloting," and "shunting." The "bank" engine-men wait with their engines in steam, coaled, and watered, near to the passenger-station; and should an engine-man come up with a disabled engine, he hooks "off," and the bank engine hooks "on," and takes the train away; and the crippled engine proceeds to the shed for repairs. Or should an engine-man come up who finds, owing to a heavy train, he is losing time, he obtains the assistance of the "bank" engine, taking it with him in front as far as he likes. He will not take the bank engine if he can avoid it, because an engine in front smothers the one behind it with dust or slush, which is apt to get into the machinery and start it heating. A bank engine-man must know his way about the line.

The pilot engine-men assist other engine-men who are strangers to the part they are about to pass over; but the term piloting is generally applied to engines which assist the goods-engines as the " bank " engine does the passenger engines. The shunting engine-men marshal the waggons and carriages about the yards and stations, and get them ready for the main-line engines to be attached to them as soon as they come out of the shed. The shunting engines reduce the hours of the main-line men, which allows them more time for rest; and, besides, it enables the train engine to get away with a fire intact. When the train engine is messing about and shunting, it pulls the fire about and causes the slag in the coal to run, which, meeting with no blast, settles upon the bars, and clinkers them over.

RAILWAY-MAN'S NEW PORTABLE GAS-LAMP.

There is a class of engine-men who have no engine, but carry a shovel and gauge-lamp, and their firemen carry two lamps. These are relievers. Some half-dozen of them occupy a cabin at the end of the passenger-platform, and in their turns they take charge of the engines from the main-line engine-men, who get straight off their engines, and walk to the steam-shed, where they enter the repairs they require in the book, and talk for a few minutes with other drivers of what they have seen and heard on the road. It is not an uncommon thing for two drivers to meet in this way, who, four hours previously, were three hundred miles apart, having come one hundred and fifty miles from opposite directions. The relief-men take charge of the engine, and put their own lamps on. The lamps and tools belonging to the engine are locked up by the fireman before he leaves it; otherwise, the next time he comes on duty he would find that somebody had taken them. The relief engine-man and his mate—they don't call him a fireman—take the engine to the turn-table, and turn it round if required, and then run it to the coal-stage, where they leave it under the charge of the turner after they have looked it round.

It is with the relievers that a young engine-man is first appointed, without an engine, and without much responsibility; he is, in fact, very kindly " let down " into his position. From this work he goes piloting, and as the best of the engines and the best of the men are on the best of the work, he finds himself in some queer company sometimes as regards engines. It is at the beginning of his career that he will be called upon to bring out all that he knows, and apply it at a moment's notice, or to act with great firmness.

Some young engine-men are very sharp and shrewd, and it is because they are filled with information, and have not to seek and to buy it when required. Others there are who start with nothing, and they end prematurely. One was piloting a passenger-train up a thirty-mile bank when his engine commenced to slip. When he shut " off " steam, the coupling lifted off the draw-bar hook; when he put on steam again, he did not notice any difference in the working of his engine, because he was " digging " into it, and so the power was expended upon his own engine in gaining speed, for he ran fifteen miles before he found out that he was detached from the train-engine.

The ear should be trained to detect, on the foot-plate, the slightest variation in the beat, so that if four carriages out of sixteen were to become detached through a coupling breaking, it would be known on the foot-plate instantly. This power of discrimination is obtained by first-class engine-men, who know exactly how sixteen carriages pull, and how much less coal it takes to pull twelve carriages. After a young driver has been piloting for a time, and the foreman finds he can get on with " old tubs," he is promoted to the position of engine-man on the goods-trains, and takes his place with other men in a link. While he is piloting with any kind of engine, and shunting in the yard, and running all over the line with specials—fish, excursions, minerals, &c.—he is not asked to account for his consumption of fuel, because it is known that his work cannot be defined or worked into figures, and it is charged to general expenses. But as soon as a young driver joins a link of men, and works with a regular engine, then his mettle is tried for the first time. He has to see what he can do—to keep the road, to keep his engine together, to keep out of collisions, to keep off the fine-list, to keep time, and to work with the least possible consumption of fuel. From a spark in the lagging of a boiler caused by a neglected ash-pan, to the wreck of an engine and train caused by neglecting *in time* a danger-signal, there are facts enough to fill a volume.

A young driver's work was once marred, as many another's has been, because he could never bring his plans to a focus, or conform them to a general scheme. His prejudices against a *system* mastered him in practice. He had had the best of information given him freely and gratuitously before he was placed upon an engine, but with such a temperament as his was, reasoning, which implies liberation from prejudice, had no fair chance. His mode of working was not the growth of thought, but was founded on likes and dislikes, which had grown up into his mind he scarcely knew how; and his strength—what he possessed—was the outcome of repetition, and not, as it should have been, deliberate examination. His engine was attached to an express, in the place of an engine that had suddenly failed with a burst tube, after having " banked " for four hours. He had proceeded fifty miles out of one hundred and twenty miles when he smelled something warming, which caused him of course to leave the foot-plate and walk on to the engine-framing, when he found the lagging was on fire; that is, the woodwork underneath the sheet-iron casing which is placed round the boiler. He was under obligation to keep good time, and what with the fire and

speed, he was not in a comfortable position on a very dark night. He and his fireman endeavoured to put the fire out with buckets of water, and while they were fully occupied endeavouring to do so, they missed the distant-signal of a station, but fortunately sighted the home-signal in time to stop at the station, when the locomotive superintendent, who happened to be there, saw the state they were in. He examined the ash-pan, which he found nearly full of ashes, which of course rolled out and had been struck by the big-end, and carried up into the dilapidated portions of the cleading, so causing the fire. The engine-man was severely censured, and was put back to firing; all this entirely through his not doing what he had every chance and opportunity of performing, and should have performed. This is a full-length portrait of a driver who kicks over his traces by refusing to learn from his authorities, and who cares nothing for any definite system of working.

Little better was the case of driver Pinder, who was running goods, and in a fair way for higher service. He came on duty one night without examining the Special Notice board, which is supplementary to the General Notice board, on which are posted notices to engine-men, intended to be reminders of some duties as binding as those in their rule-books, though the special notices are supposed to be annulled when taken down. A notice was on the board when Pinder came on duty, that the incessant rain had swollen a river so much as to have rendered a bridge, over which he would have to cross with his train, dangerous; that until further notice it would be worked as a single line; and that a pilot-man was appointed to pass the train over it after each driver had brought his train to a stand-still. Pinder had neglected to read the special notices, and, therefore, was unaware of his danger until too late. Approaching the bridge at an ordinary speed, he ought first to have seen a red light; whether he did see it or not is uncertain, but as the pilot-man was at the other end of the bridge, he could not warn the driver, who ran with his train right into a gap, and into the river below, and he and his fireman were killed on the spot. Many minor accidents have occurred by neglecting the Notice board—such as running into the work of platelayers who were relaying rails. This mishap occurred to a driver who was young in experience, and who was an extra engine-man, and one in whom his foreman had great confidence. A notice was posted on the board that, at a certain place, all drivers running over that portion of the line, must look out for signals as the surface-men or platelayers were changing the rails. Rowland, the driver, was sent in charge of an excursion-train over this road, and as he neglected the board, he was not aware of the alteration; consequently, he was unprepared to stop, and ran by the out-look man, and went off the road with his engine and three carriages. A very singular notice was once put upon a board respecting a pair of crossing-gates which were attended to in the day by a man, and in the night mostly by his wife. The old man was accidentally run over and killed, and the railway authorities, in consideration of his past duties and unfortunate end, were disposed to allow the widow to mind them in the day, and to have them closed at night, and opened by the drivers. It was a single line and only three trains passed through them between eight P.M. and six A.M. The notice was there for all to read, but about a dozen gates were demolished before all the drivers whom it concerned *really knew* of it.

We have already considered the reason why one driver's ill-success is no caution to another, and it is a great cause for comfort to reflect that the experienced officials of railways have recognised this to be a natural and permanent truth.

Classify the passenger drivers, and you will find sufficient difference to satisfy you that the worst half is composed of men who have had no experience on the goods-trains, and that *unthinking* men do learn alone from their own experience. If a man is promoted from the position of a fireman to that of a passenger driver, he will, as sure as gospel, find out on passenger-trains what it is to choke a fire; to get off the road in " trap " points; to overshoot signals; to find out he has left half a train behind him; to have a dirty, unworkable screw-jack on the tender; to have a worn-out brake screw. These irregularities, which almost all learn from experience to avoid, will become known to him at the expense of many vexatious delays and complaints from passengers. The growing importance of the passenger traffic makes it popular, and therefore only the brightest men, possessing the pure essence of enginemanship, can work it with any chance of success.

Some drivers shut off steam when approaching a station half a mile farther off than others, and as the momentum of the train represents so much stored-up energy derived ultimately from the fuel in the fire-box, it is delivered by running the half-mile without steam. A driver, say, makes forty stops a day, and shuts off steam at each station half a mile sooner than he is accustomed to do. He runs twenty miles with the steam "off; " whereas formerly he was burning fuel and wearing brake-blocks and wheels out, in order to stop where the stored-up energy of the train would have taken him, without making a second of difference in time.

After an engine-man has been on the goods service for a number of years, and has become well acquainted with engines of various kinds, he begins to look for promotion. This is regulated in many sheds in the order of seniority, but sometimes a bad history keeps a man back; for every time a man figures on the fine-sheet for an offence, it is registered in the books against him for the remainder of his term, and if he lets out a word about promotion, the " history " is produced against him, and he may fare badly, too, if it should read thus:—

Fined, one day's pay for choking a fire, and losing forty-five minutes.

Fined, one day's pay for hanging a hook upon the safety-valve lever.

Fined, two pounds, for locking the safety-valves of his engine.

Fined, one day's pay, for stopping on the road to clean the tubes.

Fined, one day's pay, for running through a pair of gates.

Fined, one day's pay, for threatening to throw his fireman off the engine.

SCENE OF THE ACCIDENT AT WINCHBURGH, ON THE EDINBURGH AND GLASGOW RAILWAY.

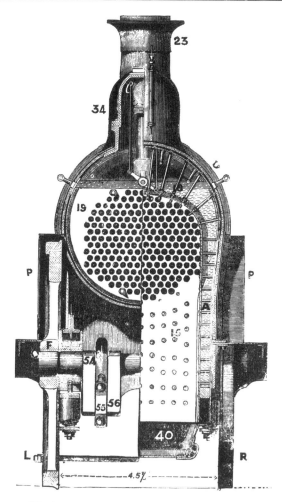

"The Grosvenor." Cross Sections.
15. Stays in walls of fireboxes. 18. Ditto from crown plate to covering-plate. 19. Tubes. 23. Chimney Cap. 40. Ash-pan. 54. Crank-Shaft. 55. Big End. 56. Arm of Big End. 34. Dome. A. Water Space. F. Nave of Wheel. PP. Splashers over Driving Wheels. R. Right Side of Engine. L. Left Ditto.

Fined, one pound, for having a stranger on the engine.

Fined, half-a-crown, for smoke nuisance.

Fined, five shillings, for bringing a pig 150 miles without permission.

Fined, one shilling, for breaking a coupling.

Fined, a day's pay, for running over three horses, and not reporting it.

While an engine-man is on the goods service he is exposed to more temptations than dangers; but unless the guard is a confederate, there is very little chance of thieving. It has happened that two bottles of brandy have been found on the engine, or a lot of fish, or a new pair of boots. Men have been taken-up for having fowl, ducks, and green peas in their baskets. When fowls were missing, they generally "walked off" in couples, as they did of old into the Ark. But, considering the amount of property in transit, and considering the facilities men have for helping themselves, while shunting in a siding to clear the way for passenger-trains, it must be acknowledged that they are, on the whole, a straightforward, honest body of men.

With regard to the dangers attending goods drivers, they, of all railway men, are the safest. Their speed is not very high, and, therefore, if there is anything on the line that they can see, they have ample time to stop before it; but, in the dark, they fare much better than anybody on the main line, because they are timed to keep time, and if they don't, which is often the case, they cannot trip anybody else up. But the *high-fliers* —expresses—come into the tail of their train sometimes with a crash, which may be by the length of from forty to sixty waggons distant from the goods driver, who can afford to jump off his engine, and ask the "flier" what he thinks of doing. "If thou thinks to get first," said one goods driver to an express man, who was engine-deep amongst the débris of a dozen waggons, "thou'st better back out, and thou go round Colwick;" which was a route fifty miles away.

By the time a driver has served five or seven years on the goods trains, there is, or should be, very little to be in ignorance of, for in that time he will have had every opportunity of knowing *all* that is to be known about an engine—firing, driving, and the general management of it, for there has been a multitude of chances.

Promotion from the goods-trains to the passenger-trains is very welcome, for it is a deliverance from long hours, and from the anxious duty of keeping clear of fast trains, and from the cold and poisonous damp air of night. Calamities may follow for he will not be clear of them; but, having been taught in a good Spartan school, by hard lessons and a rough life, he will be able to grapple with them. If he has divorced himself from the idea that there is such a thing as chance upon a railway, he will not slacken for fear, nor be struck by colour-blindness through looking to see if a fire is burning rightly; nor will there be a silent terror in the mind to whisper of hidden dangers. No! He will run along like flame, and will handle the regulator with an arm whose inspiration is experience. The recollection of the past has taught him that everything is consequent, and nothing comes by a chance. Neglecting to look after a little steel pin—a trivial thing, some may be inclined to think—and yonder magnificent iron steed, champing and foaming under steam, is imminently liable to an accident, that will reveal the character of the driver. Neglect the working of a trimming—but a few strands of worsted, some may think—and the steel-crank journal will grip an axle-box, and wrench it out of the framing. Neglect yonder small red light, and the engine, with a train, is wrecked. Neglect the undeviating plan of nature in combustion, and the fire is choked. Neglect small things, and doubt their power, and the engine will be stopped, even by a grain of sand in the packing, by one strand of worsted too many, by a shovelful of coal too much, by the flaw in a leaf of a spring, by a false stroke of the pump, by a slip of the wheel, by a loose cotter, for the want of one spot of oil, one glance at the gauge-glass, heedlessness of a single notice.

On the slow passenger-trains a driver has a very fair berth; his engine is prepared for him, cleaned, and lighted up, and he is in charge to run from station to station; he is, in fact, in

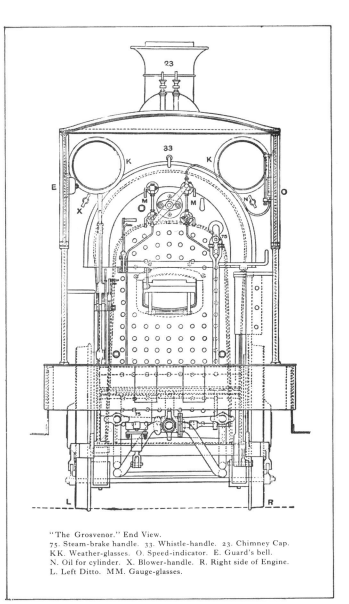

"The Grosvenor." End View.
75. Steam-brake handle. 33. Whistle-handle. 23. Chimney Cap. KK. Weather-glasses. O. Speed-indicator. E. Guard's bell. N. Oil for cylinder. X. Blower-handle. R. Right side of Engine. L. Left Ditto. MM. Gauge-glasses.

training for higher speed, for longer runs without a stop, to be performed day after day. Each feature of passenger working is stamped upon his mind, and he finds that with passenger-trains there is much to be learned to keep time, and to steer clear of danger. It is not so much knowledge of engines that he is supposed to possess, as a knowledge of the running at a higher speed of more important trains.

On the fast passenger-trains, a driver's good name and fame depend upon three things, viz., a thorough good fire well burned through before starting, a thorough good examination of his engine before joining a train, a thorough and constant look-out for signals.

The peculiar character of express working is favourable to observation. The driver keeps the same engine for years, and gets acquainted with all its peculiarities, and therefore he can manage that engine—his own—better than another. He runs the same trains, and past the same signals; he uses pretty regularly the same class of coal, so that he can catch with a quick eye the slightest deviation from the common current of events. All these things create a sense of fitness and strength for his post; he is swift in proportion to his knowledge of the road and its varying gradients. There can be nothing shadowy in the recollection of it; all misgivings are rolled away; and in the struggle to keep time, to give public satisfaction, to injure no one, he knows to an inch and to an instant where and when to stop. Discord and confusion underly all railway working, but the rightly-prepared mind and eye can steer through the vague mass of points, and traps, and gullets, and signals, and tunnels.

But these Philistines of high speed that come and go in our day are more fortunate than the earlier drivers, who had to stand upon foot-plates with no weather-board to protect them, and no block-system to keep them from jostling together. There were scarcely any tail-lights to the trains, and signals were not easily seen, being fixed up by side of a wood, or where the drivers had to stop very nearly to find them. So far as the speed of engines is concerned, we have not been able to improve upon them much. We ran sixty miles an hour thirty years ago, and that speed is seldom exceeded even now with all our accumulated experience. But speed is now maintained under more favourable conditions, and for longer distances.

We have the finest locomotives in the world; and for comfort far before anything that old engine-men in their firing days could have dreamed of. The outline may be somewhat the same as of old, but the details of our present engines have been wrought out with consummate skill. We remember having to oil some of the old grandfathers of the present engines; and a fine job it was. It required a special oil-can and a torch lamp; and, to oil the big-ends and excentrics, a fellow had to screw his head and body into an incalculably small compass, and screw out again with a black patch of grease on a clean slop. A good deal of tallow was used in big-ends, and the axle-boxes were made so that you could *not* get at the trimmings.

New ideas have come to the front with new men, and there is more of art and less of tinkering to be seen, so that the locomotive has become a mechanical achievement of the highest order.

On all the great railway systems, the object sought is to get over more ground in less time, which is partially attained by taking " stops " off, and running through-trains, and by hooking to those trains engines capable of maintaining the speed under the direction of highly experienced drivers. The first improvement towards quick travelling was achieved by laying down a trough between the rails, from which the drivers could pick up water whilst running—an idea of great value, brought out by the eminent locomotive engineer, Mr. Ramsbottom.

The water is pumped from a well into the troughs by a small steam-engine fixed by the side of the railway. As soon as the engine is over the trough, a scoop is lowered by the fireman into the water, by means of a lever worked from the foot-plate. The scoop being dipped into the water, which is of course stationary, the speed of the engine onwards causes the water to run up the scoop into the tender, which is very soon filled up; after which the fireman raises the scoop out of the water. Occasionally, this process has not been unattended by some irregularity, followed by no trifling amount of discomfort to the men.

On one occasion, as the fireman attempted to shut off the water, he found it was impossible to do so completely, and therefore the water continued to rise; and before the engine reached the end of the trough all the coal had been washed out of the tender, together with the shovel. It was dark at the time, and the fire-door was opened to give the fireman a light on to the tank-lid, so that he could see when the tender was full; and as he could not raise the scoop, the water came over instantly and washed the coals direct into the fire-box, filling it over the brick arch. The train was the "limited" mail, and therefore the men were determined to make the best of it. They had one thing in their favour, and that was a boiler full of water, and a favourable gradient before them for thirty miles. The shovel having gone, the fireman scraped the coal away from the door with his hands, and every effort had to be made to bring round the fire, which was nearly extinguished. They succeeded in reaching their first stopping place with only a few minutes' delay. They borrowed a shovel and trimmed the fire up, and before they arrived at their destination they had recovered the lost time.

THE COVERED WAY LEADING TO THE PLATFORMS AT CHARING CROSS STATION, LONDON.

CHAPTER IV

IT sometimes happens that no extent of experience and study of railway working can prepare a man for any occurrence that happens on the railway. There swoops down upon a man at times a surprise, the like of which has not visited any one before; and, quick as lightning, the greatest evil or the greatest good is done on the spur of the moment. An occurrence of this kind once fell to the lot of an old and experienced driver, in charge of an express-train going north. The train left the Metropolis at its proper time, and was running under full steam, when the driver suddenly saw a goods-train crossing the line in front of him. He could not stop within the distance for want of brake-power. He remained on the engine almost to the last, but not three seconds could have elapsed between the sailing along, in all the majesty of power, and entering the eternal world. Both driver and fireman decided to jump and brave accidents. One leaped on the right side of the engine and the other on the left, but the train passed on between their lifeless bodies. They were dead; both of them. The engine rushed into the goods-train, and cut waggon after waggon out before she stopped, and then she was upright and almost uninjured, and none of the passengers were killed.

There is a speed bordering upon instantaneous death, resolving fate at once; but scores of engine-men have jumped and injured themselves, whereas if they had remained on their engines they would have been unhurt. In collisions like the above-mentioned, it required more than human judgment to decide what is the best thing to do. If we take the case of the accident to the Irish Mail at Abergele, we find the fireman in the débris and the fire, burned to a heap of ashes; and the driver, who jumped off to save his life, so injured that he survived the shock only two weeks. Now, in the Sittingbourne accident, the engine plunged into the trucks at about thirty miles an hour, and scattered them right and left; but the driver and the fireman were carried on their engine safe through them, although several passengers were mortally injured. The accident occurred in broad daylight, and the engine-man and the fireman had time and opportunity to jump, but they chose to remain. It is impossible to advise what to do under such circumstances. Had the Sittingbourne trucks contained oil, like those at Abergele, the men would have been burned to death! and, on the other hand, if they had jumped off at thirty miles an hour, the chances are that both would have broken their necks.

A case occurred on one of our principal railways at night, which alarmed the driver very much. Had it happened in daylight it would have cost him his life. He was steaming south, with an express-train of eighteen carriages, at forty miles an hour, and, when passing a junction, he struck four trucks, and sent them flying, not only clear of his road, but clear of both roads. The waggons had been shunted on to the main-line by mistake,

CLEARING THE WRECKAGE AFTER THE ACCIDENT AT BERWICK.

ACCIDENT AT WENNINGTON, NEAR LANCASTER, TO A MIDLAND RAILWAY TRAIN.

just as the express came up, and therefore they were in motion, which accounts for the engine buffer-beam being comparatively uninjured. The collision was so sudden, that before the driver and the fireman knew what had happened, all was over. The engine knocked beams, diagonals, and axles in a tempest, clear of her course, and would have continued; but, of course, the driver stopped, whilst the rear-guard was ignorant of what had happened. Now, the driver declares he should have jumped had this occurred in broad daylight. We have the Sittingbourne accident, in which the engine-man was safe at high speed. *But*, although it is the safest plan to keep to the engine, one never knows what the trucks contain. As not one truck out of ten thousand contains oil or gunpowder, we may conclude from experience that, in cases of pending collisions, it is best to remain on the foot-plate.

A driver of a fast express collided with a goods-train in a curve. The goods-train had stopped within the distant-signal, and the signalman neglected to protect it in time. He, in fact, was not at his post when the goods-train arrived, ten minutes behind time. The train should have been in the siding, shunted clear for the express. The express-driver, having a thorough knowledge of the traffic, as well as of his engine, expected to pass it at this particular spot. On sighting the distant-signal, it indicated line clear, by exhibiting a clear, white light. When he came into the curve, he saw the three red lights on the end of the goods-guard's van, and, even then, he thought the goods must be in the siding, and that the guard had neglected to change his tail-lights from red to white. He had shut off steam, having a doubt of the position of the goods, when the flying steed went right inside of the van, and a fair slaughter of waggons took place; some went flying to the right, and others to the left; and although twenty waggons were cut out of the goods-train, the express engine remained upright. She left the rails when she struck the van, and rode on bent axles, broken chains and rails, until she stopped. The buffer-beam was smashed, the chimney and smoke-box damaged, but neither the driver not fireman was hurt, and many of the passengers knew nothing of the danger they had been in.

This was an affair that took place in the dark. Had it occurred in the day, the probability is that both the driver and the fireman would have jumped, and injured themselves. Now, this was another instance in which the enginemanship avails nothing. The driver was a man who knew every train on the road, and looked out for them, and when he had passed one, he looked for another, and so on, to the end of the trip. But the accident could have been prevented by the use of the block-system which is now nearly universally adopted.

The down Scotch express was going down Retford bank, signals all clear, when Oliver Hindly saw a train going east from Sheffield to Lincoln which would meet him on the level crossing. He could not stop, and with that clear mind which is so marked in Englishmen in time of danger, he put on full steam, and sent Mr. Sturrock's beautiful express-engine clean through the goods-train, scattering the trucks like match splinters and carrying all through safe. When asked about the matter, Hindly said he could not keep clear, so he would clear away his obstruction. There is no doubt that had he hesitated or feared many lives would have been sacrificed. No. 210 engine carried the dents and scars like an old warrior, and looked handsomer than ever for this brush with the enemy of express-trains.

The principle of the block-system is this: the signalman must not allow two trains on the line between his cabin and the cabin of the next signalman in advance. Signalman A telegraphs to signalman B to know whether the line is clear; and, having received an affirmative answer, he allows the train to pass his cabin and approach that of B, and when it has passed him, he informs A of the circumstance. If the train goes on all right, he will tell him so; if it stopped at his cabin, he would wire line blocked; and A would hold back the next train that comes on. He could hold on to one, because he would wire to the man who sent him the train, line blocked; and when that had got another train, he would hold that back, and wire to the man who sent it, line blocked; so that, in case of serious failure, one train may have been stopped at each signal cabin over a length of

fifty miles. But, notwithstanding all the precautions on the part of the railway directors to make their line safe by working on the block-system, the best of rolling stock on most solid of tracks, accidents will happen. Soon after the block-system was introduced on railways, a signalman had sent on a goods-train to the next signalman, and an express-train being due, he was anxious to obtain the signal clear. The goods were a long time on the road, the night was dark and wild, and lightning was vivid and frequent, accompanied by loud peals of thunder. Now, lightning affects telegraph instruments. The indication of " line clear " was at that time given by *one* ring on a bell. The signalman was looking out very anxiously for this ring, for the express was due, and there is always a bother about stopping or even checking an express. All at once a flash of lightning ripped down an oak tree by the side of his cabin; and the electric fluid, acting like the battery, rung the bell. The train was near, down went all the signals, and on went the train right into the goods-train. The guard's-van of the goods had a lamp in the centre of the roof, and when the passenger struck the van, the lamp was projected into the air, and then fell down on to the engine foot-plate between the driver and fireman, with such a crash that they thought it was a thunderbolt, and both jumped off unhurt. Here was a lesson! " Line clear," and other messages, are given by two or more distinct rings.

Sweet are the uses of difficulties, for they develop character and bring to the fore the capacious powers which lie folded up in a man, sometimes to such an extent that an individual is half-scared at his own daring. Driver Brewood was in charge of a goods-train, consisting of twenty-four waggons of Aberdare coal. There was a bank to descend of 1 in 80 for five miles; then a level to run over of one mile, and then another bank of 1 in 85 for a length of six miles, which terminated at a meeting station. The line was a single line, and trains coming in opposite directions passed by means of sidings at the appointed meeting station. Before the train was started from the top of the first incline, it was customary to put some, if not all, the brakes down, so as to enable the driver and the guard to control the train.

One very dark night the driver received the " right-away " signal, and he started. All went well until he reached the level between the two inclines. The fireman generally handles the brake, and keeps easing it "on" or "off" as circumstances require. When they reached the level, Brewood was struck by the speed being so soon reduced, and at first thought the guards had put all the brakes down in the train; so he took hold of the tender-brake, and after giving it a turn of the screw he found he stopped the train. In an instant he turned it off, and put on steam. He knew he had broken away, and the regulator and engine soon informed him he had but a few trucks behind his engine. He went over the back of the tender and on to the waggons. He found he had four, and he returned, and hastened down the second incline to the meeting station where he was timed to pass the " Black " goods. They ran into the siding, the points of course being set to receive them. After he stopped, he sent his fireman to meet the trucks which had broken away. At the top of the yard, the black goods stopped to put off trucks; but misfortune never comes alone, they were not there or in sight. Brewood rushed to the station-master's house door, and with a huge stick unmercifully hammered into one unfortunate panel until the official threw wide open his bed-room door, and was going to remonstrate, but the driver lost no time. " For God's sake come out, there are twenty waggons of coal coming down the bank like the devil. I can hear, by the Lord Harry, there will be a smash. Come out quick." The station-master slipped on his pants and socks, and out he came with his nightcap on. " What can we do ? " gasped Brewood. " Why, turn all the lot into the river below," said the frightened agent running to meet the train; adding, in hot haste, " Look sharp with the hammer, Brewood, and we shall have time to spike the back road points." Just as they drove in the spike, Brewood sprung into a pile of chairs, and shouted, " Bring a few iron chairs." They laid them across the metals as near as they dared, and off they ran

out of danger. The waggons drove over the chairs, and then followed a crash. The first two dropped into the ballast and formed a stop-buffer for the others, and none went into the river. The driver and the agent ran to the débris, to look for the guards, but the guards and their van were nowhere to be seen. In the darkness they could hear it coming.

The two guards in the rear noticed on the level between the two inclines that they were going rather too fast, but they did not notice it until the train had obtained a very high speed for the weight. All doubts about the matter were soon dispelled. They knew that they had broken away from the engine, and what alarmed them was the fear that the driver did not know it, and not hearing the engine whistle they were both of opinion that their train would overtake him, and so they expected every minute to be smashed. To jump at that speed was certain death. They knew what could be, and what might be, but they did not know what would be. They were for once with their lives in their hands. The black goods would be in the station, and Brewood in the siding, and there was no other course but to turn them into the back road, and that meant into the river. Like men with death staring them in the face, they made an effort for dear life, resolved not to surrender it without a desperate struggle. With the lamps glimmering in the weird darkness they clambered from truck to truck to put down more brakes. They did this like heroes, but the momentum of the waggons gave them no hope of stopping them. They had done all that they could, and it was plain that a dreadful collision would take place. The head guard thought the black goods might set back, and give the run-away trucks time to stop on the level; " but I shall jump, mate, if we meet a red light, because that will show that they have done all they can, and that still there is danger." " If we jump," replied the under guard, " we shall be killed dead on the spot." " What is it to be, jump or not ? " shouted the other. " Jump, mate, good-bye," and each went to jump; but when men are in such a trying position the falchion of the intellect cuts into the scabbard of the brain. " Here, mate," shouted the head guard, " we are saved. Bring that hammer out of the locker, sharp." He himself took up a shackle hook, and knocked a hole into the end of the van over the coupling; and, with life and death in sight, the under guard eased off the van-brake, and the head guard knocked the bolt out which attached the truck next them to the van: and they were living men. They had scarcely become free before they saw the fireman's light, and they pulled up to pick him up. The van being on the incline it would start by the force of gravitation. When they came to the débris they saw what a tremendous hit it was to hook off. " I assure you," said the head guard to Brewood, " it was the thought of an instant, prompted by the instinct of self-preservation. I suppose when the wheel of fortune comes off, it stirs a man up a bit. I have been on the railway close upon twelve years, and in that time I have been knocked all round the van, but I never had an escape like this. Hooking off the van was simply a divine interposition of providence." They left the van where they had stopped it, and walked to the trucks; and, whatever was in fortune's power, they all saw each had had his share that night. There may be storms at sea for sailors, but it is quite certain that a sight presented itself that convinced them that on the railway there are perils for engine-men, firemen, and guards.

An occurrence that took place a few years ago will illustrate the importance of railway men being always on the alert to act upon incidental hints which at first sight appear uncommon. A goods-train, having two engines attached, was proceeding south at midnight, and after it had passed a fast express-train, a thought struck the driver of the express train that for two engines it was a very short goods-train. He stepped over to the fireman's side of the foot-plate for the purpose of seeing whether there were any tail-lights on the last vehicle; but owing to a curve in the line, he could not ascertain that point. He, however, shut off steam, and gave instructions to his mate to have the brake in readiness, " for," said he, " it strikes me very forcibly, mate, all the train is not there." When they had run about two miles, and were thinking of getting up the speed again, a red light was seen ahead surging violently from right to left. They pulled up at once to it, when a goods guard informed them that a waggon-axle had broken in his train, and had caused twelve trucks to leave the rails, and that they were across the down-road right in the way of the express.

The guard got up on the step of the engine, when they pulled gently down to the scene of the accident, where they saw that it requires heads that think and eyes that roll, as well as simply engine-men, to make railway-men of.

AN INQUEST JURY VISITING THE SCENE OF A RAILWAY ACCIDENT.

SCENE OF THE RECENT ACCIDENT IN THE SOUTH OF IRELAND.

CHAPTER V.

PUNISHMENT AND ITS ADMINISTRATION.

THE administration of punishment on a railway, which is a little state, is a serious duty. Without punishment, there would be a total loss of power and of salutary influences. Offences may be classed under the heads of breach of rules, repeated disobedience, constant idleness, bullying, gross insubordination, and, worst of all, drink. A driver of goods-trains, out for very long hours, gets tired, has to wait long for a passenger-train to pass, yields to the temptation, and goes into a public-house, with guards, traders, drovers, and others; and in time is sure to come to grief. He is wanted, and is not there; or his engine gets short of water and the fire is low. All at once, the signal " right away " is given, and Driver Unstable is off; and when he sticks on the bank short of steam and water, he begins to repent that Dick Easy got him into the beer-shop.

In dealing with offenders, it is necessary to consider not their services, but their dispositions, and the general welfare of all. Punishment does not amount to dismissal unless the delinquent is an hardened offender. Dismissal is a serious matter, for justice herself makes a marked distinction between wilfully bad conduct and thoughtlessness. The real sting of punishment should lie in the fact that it has been sought for. There is no disgrace in being punished for what one never had any thought or intention of doing. The idea of such punishment is repulsive in the sense of right and wrong; and when the mistake is made, the individual becomes a martyr, not an offender.

Then, again, punishment is to be administered with the greatest care, with a knowledge of human nature; for, what would break one man's heart, might be felt by that of another but lightly. Or, it may even harden the heart when the punishment is inflicted in anger, or vindictively, or for temporary revenge, or for self-interest, or for applause. The creed upon which punishment is inflicted should rest upon a purely rational basis.

With regard to the imposition of fines, it may be laid down as a general maxim, that it should be of such a nature as to do some positive good. The sting of punishment has been inflicted by some superintendents in a novel way.

Driver Sparrow was always—that is to say, oftener than others—before the board of inquiry, consisting of the locomotive superintendent and his assistants. The man's offences were not marked by gross insubordination, but repeated instances of thoughtlessness. He would run short of coals, simply because he was afraid to take too much. His notion of coal was peculiar. No, he would not have a bit more; he would try to make what he had in the tender last him. The consequence was that, on several occasions, he had to make a special stop with his train to get a few hundredweights more; and, on one occasion, when some of the officials were in the train, instead of stopping to take in fuel, he burned the tool-boxes, and all the old clothes in them, and several pounds of tallow, together with the lid of the tender, and the footboard, which just saved his bacon. On another occasion he stopped at a country road-side station and borrowed some coals. For this he was fined a day's pay. The next time, he stopped by the side of a waggon of coal which he spied on the road, and helped himself from it. He took the number of the waggon and reported the case. He never tried to hide anything, and he did things as calmly as possible. The guard would shout, "What are you stopping here for?" "Oh!" Sparrow would reply; "I have got a bit of bad coal in my tender, and this 'ere is tidy good; give us a hand a minute." It was against all rules and regulations to delay a train for such a purpose, and he was fined again, and made pay for the coals, which belonged to a coal merchant. He again ran short of coals and helped himself from a waggon, the proprietor of which desired to charge him with stealing them. He got into much trouble. The case was allowed to proceed a certain length, to frighten Sparrow; and it had the desired effect. Fortunately, with all scheming for coal, he had never taken a coal premium; or the coal-merchant would have had all his own way, and Jack Sparrow would have been "caged" for a time. Strange to relate, he no sooner left off one class of thoughtless acts, than he betook himself to another class—not minding his time-table properly, calling where he should not, and running past where he should have stopped—offences which generally occurred on the first day of the month. At a certain station where he had not been in the habit of calling, seeing the passengers he shut off steam and stopped. "Fetch that time-bill, mate. By Gom, them's our passengers," said he. The time-bill was consulted, but he found they were not. A little further he saw another group of passengers at a station. Those he took no notice of; but, when he stopped at the station beyond that, the agent asked him if he stopped at Slade Heath. "No," said he. "But," replied the agent, "you should have done. What am I to do? I have neither an engine nor a carriage to fetch them, and you must go on. You have put me and them into a fix." However, the agent had to consider what was the best thing to do, and by telegraph he found that there were eight passengers. The distance was five miles; he sent a waggonette for them, and Sparrow had to pay for their ride.

His next offence was to take a gentleman twenty miles beyond his destination, whom he was told to set down at a certain place. It was the last train at night, and Sparrow had to pay the gentleman's hotel bill. He turned up again for having two gentlemen on his engine one night with the mail, for which he paid two sovereigns—the regular fine. Next, he started away from a station without looking back, and left the rear guard behind. The head guard gave the signal; but it is the duty of the driver to look back, after starting, in order to see if any passenger may be jumping out. This frequently happens; passengers sit still during the time the train is at the station, and when it is on the move they think of asking if that is such a station; and finding it is the very station they want, they frequently jump out, or rather tumble out, even when the train is going ten or fifteen miles an hour.

To Sparrow once more; and this is the climax, all through not looking back. He backed on to a train; and in time he received the all-right signal to go. Sparrow had noticed a travelling official on the platform. When he arrived at the first station where he was timed to stop, a porter was sweeping the platform with a broom, professionally to and fro. "Look out, my lad, he's in here," said Sparrow pantomimically, with his thumb cocked up and his fingers closed, as plainly as his fist could speak.—"Ah! ha!" cried the lad, "not him; thou hast got no carriages." Sure enough he had not; and, incredible as it may appear, he had run six miles without looking back, or finding out by the working of the engine that he had left his train behind.

What could be done with such a man? "Discharge him," some would have exclaimed. But, with all his faults, he broke no bones or waggons, nor neglected his engine, nor absented himself. He had reached his climax, and the best thing to do was to forgive him for this, and inform him that for the next offence he must take his discharge.

"You quite understand," said the superintendent to him, "that your term of service ends with your next offence. I have no more to say to you; the time of your stay in the company's service is in your own hands, when you think proper to 'snuff' yourself out. Your back week's pay will be paid you by making an application to the time-keeper." Sparrow is running now, and has been running for years since he left the train behind, and got the option of "snuffing" himself out any minute.

To forgive an offence has, on some natures, a beneficial influence. In this case it secured the services of a steady driver for years.

Some very strange cases are sometimes inquired into and dealt with according to their merits.

An express-train, in charge of two smart men, was travelling at forty-five miles an hour, when the engine became uncoupled from the tender. It happened when the fireman was on the tender breaking up some coal. They coupled them together again, and neither the guard nor passengers knew it; and it would never have been known had not some farm labourers, who saw the engine shoot away from the tender, have narrated the circumstance in a neighbouring town, where a station-master heard it. He reported the talk to head-quarters, from whence instructions were issued to inquire into the case. When the right driver was found, after some difficulty, he did not deny it. Both he and his fireman were summoned to appear before the board of inquiry, and full particulars were obtained of all the circumstances.

It appeared that when they were going at speed, the coupling-pin, which unites the engine to the tender, broke, and they separated. The engine shooting ahead broke the side links, and pulled the feed-bags out, leaving the fireman on the tender. They saw at once how matters stood with them, and the fireman was going to put the tender-brake on; but the driver ordered him to allow the train to run, and fetch a spare coupling-pin

from the back of the tool-box. By the time the fireman had done this, and lifted up the flap of the tender, the engine was under control, and was, in a trice, buffer to buffer with the tender. When all was made ready for the coupling-pin to be dropped in, the engine was sharply reversed against the momentum of the train, sufficiently to extend the draw-bar spring, and they succeeded in getting in the pin.

The mishap took place when they had run seventy-five miles out of the eighty-five miles; and, the boiler being fairly supplied with water, they managed without turning on the feed. After they stopped, every exertion was made to put the feed-bags right and square; and, as there had not been any delay, they thought the whole affair was squared, and therefore they thought there was no need to make a report of it. No one knew anything of it but themselves, and if they had told the guard, he would have made a mountain of a mouse, and sent in a report a yard long to his superintendent, which would come round to their "governor," and from him to their foreman, and from him to them. So, saving all this reporting, they would have succeeded in smothering the affair, but for the peasant's astonishment at seeing an engine bolt away from

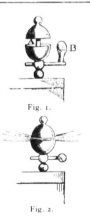

At that extremity of the engine at which the engineer stands, is placed the whistle, whose shrill and startling sound is so frequently heard, rousing the sleeper from his rest, and startling, at times, even the most stoical traveller. Fig. 1 represents this part of the apparatus when not in action. It consists of two hemispheres of brass; the upper, which is solid, being attached to the stem A, while the lower cylinder is partially hollow. By turning the handle B, the upper hemisphere is brought close to the lower as in Fig. 2, and the same motion allows of the escape of steam, which rushing between the edges of the two hemispheres, produces the shrill sound with which we are all so well acquainted.

Fig. 1.

Fig. 2.

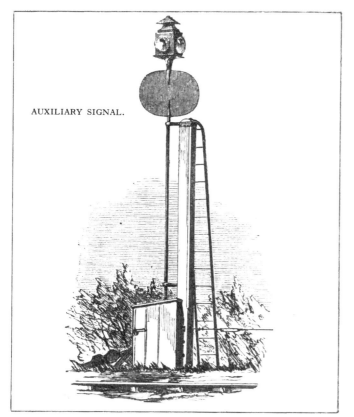

AUXILIARY SIGNAL.

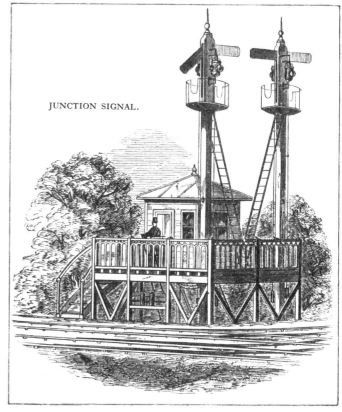

JUNCTION SIGNAL.

the tender and the train, and seeing the driver jockey his engine as they never saw before. It was a very smart piece of work—too smart to be recognised. They were advised not to do so again. Under such exceptional circumstances it is much better to stop.

Not experience alone, but judgment also, is required to grapple with railway difficulties; and one cannot get together too much information respecting what others have done, and what others have omitted to do. A general of renown, whenever he was

out walking in times of peace, was in the habit of speculating how he would marshal his soldiers to take places which attracted his notice, and how he would make a retreat, in case of being defeated, with the smallest loss to his army.

It is this kind of forethought which helps railway-men. The want of it sometimes helps them and their waggons to grief. A driver of a goods-train, consisting of thirty-five waggons and the brake-van, was proceeding one dark night over a piece of road infested with inclines; now 1 in 80 *up*, then 1 in

HAND SIGNALS.

Men required to give Hand Signals are provided with Red, Green, and White Flags, and a Signal Lamp, with Red, Green, and White Glasses, and with Fog Signals; but in any emergency, when not provided with those means of signalling, the following are adopted, namely,—

The ALL RIGHT SIGNAL is shown by extending the arm horizontally, so as to be distinctly seen by the Engine-driver, thus—

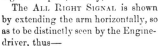

The CAUTION SIGNAL, to Proceed Slowly, is shown by one arm held straight up, thus—

The STOP SIGNAL is shown by holding both arms straight up, thus, or by waving any object with violence—

80 *down*. He had arrived at the top of one bank, when, it was supposed, the train broke asunder when it was hanging over the top of the hill. He proceeded down the hill, and thought the whole train was following him; but, when he began to climb the next hill, he found by the work of the engine that he must have broken away. He stopped, not being sure where he had left the remnant. He was no sooner on the ground than he heard the remainder of the train close upon him, and he had only just time to shout for his fireman to jump off, when it ran with tremendous force into what waggons he had, and piled them right over the engine.

Accidents similar to the above have happened with passenger-trains, through the couplings breaking when coming over a bank. It is not every driver who knows how to climb hills with a heavy train. When half of the train hangs on one side of a hill and the other half on the opposite side, it is only reasonable that the engine should be slowed after turning the hill, in order to pull the train over it without increasing the speed with which the engine arrived at the top. Many men, so soon as they reach the top of a hill, when the engine feels the power of gravitation in its favour, accelerates its speed most rapidly, thereby putting an extra strain on the couplings at the summit of the hill. Again, in running down an incline with a bank at the end, the speed should be increased before the bottom of the valley is reached by the centre of the train. Speed should be increased by giving the engine a little more steam just before reaching the valley, in order gently to pull all the couplings taut, and to run across the bottom of the valley pulling. Some men run half-way *up* a bank, taking advantage of the power of gravity acquired running down the preceding hill, before they give the engine full steam, but such men are often fined for breaking away. Then, again, men are sometimes fined for sticking on a bank with a moderate load, and delaying other trains behind them. At the same time, they insist that they had a boiler full of steam, and that the steam was even blowing-off at the time. Very true, but it is possible to have a boiler full of steam and not know how to use it. To climb a long bank with a heavy train, some men think that all that is required is a boiler blowing-off steam like "mad;" and though the engine may slip two or three times, and stick, no man, they think, can do any more, and they conclude that the load is too heavy for the engine. It is nothing of the kind. The true cause of the engine's slipping—of course we are assuming the rails are dry and not wet—is that the steam is too impulsive upon the piston: that is, it acts for a *moment* with too great a pressure, or it could not force the wheels round. If the pressure of steam be too high and you throttle it, it will accumulate in the steam-chest until it is too much for the adhesion of the wheels, and hence slipping. Now instead of the engine blowing-off steam, she should rather be inclined to be short of steam, so that the lever can be placed well over, and the regulator full open, and that the steam can be allowed to push the piston nearly to the end of the stroke, following it up with an even pressure, instead of thumping the piston with high-pressure steam and knocking the wheels round. To climb a bank with a heavy load, have the lever well over, and the regulator well open, and the steam so low that the pressure on the piston does not exceed what is required for tractive power; and as the bank is climbed, lift the damper or close the door, for more steam and more power, but leave the lever and regulator alone, unless absolutely necessary.

By such management many a man has been saved from being fined for slipping on a bank. To slip on dry rails shows distinctly that the engine-man does not know his business. Should the engine slip, drop the damper until the pressure in the cylinders becomes insufficient to slip the wheels, though sufficient to draw the train. The slipping of wheels on a bank, or in starting from a station, is produced by one and the same cause; but the engine requires different treatment, as already shown.

Over-shooting signals, or mistaking signals, is considered about as serious an offence as a man can commit, because no one can have made the mistake without having failed for the moment in his duty of taking all necessary care of his train. But, in numerous instances, the offence is committed through the wonderful elasticity of action encouraged by familiarity.

Some of the most experienced drivers have come to grief through their habits having become set. Now the sure way to avoid running by signals is to forget that the signal has ever been seen before, and to maintain day after day the same anxiety to sight it as was done in the first instance, or when we first run past it.

Half the signals which are passed, and the collisions which occur through running by them, happen by the drivers not looking out for the signals in time. A man may run over a road and find a distant-signal always "off" for him at some road-side station, until he has lost sight of it, excepting just a glance; and he may not give that glance in time on an occasion when, of all others, he should have seen it, and, before he can stop at it, he is in collision with another train. Not because the signal could not be seen from a long distance off, but the familiarity of seeing it off so many times, for so many years, has brought with it indifference. Approach every signal, and sight every signal, as though it had never been visible before, and run the road every day as carefully as at first; then the fine-sheet will be a blank for cases of over-running danger-signals.

A signal half "off" and half "on" is very often a tempting trap for a man who is in haste to form an opinion about it. It should there and then be treated as doubtful; there should be no whistling or time lost in testing it; the steam should be shut off, and if there is any delay through it, then the defective signal should have the blame. Some scores of men have been fined, and have brought their department into trouble, by endeavouring to be too clever in distinguishing right from wrong, when the truth was only known in the signal-box, and not on the foot-plate. For over-shooting signals, nothing will save an engine-man from being discharged except a clear good-conduct bill.

But that will not save a man from burning a boiler; though this is a rare occurrence, which only happens when extreme carelessness has prevailed on the foot-plate. It is generally brought about through the gauge-glass not working properly, and showing false water in the glass. This is caused by the top water-way into the boiler being clogged with dirt. When the waste-water cock on the gauge is open, the water runs out, and when it is closed the water from the boiler fills it again. That may be assumed to be correct; but it may be false, and a man may have his glass three-parts full of water at four o'clock, and find the lead plug go at 4.15. Nothing will per-

STATION SIGNAL WITH COTTAGE.

suade him that the boiler was short of water, and nothing will persuade his master that it was not. When the top water-way is made up, the pressure of the steam upon the water within the boiler forces it up into the glass; and so long as there is any water near the lower water-way, the water will continue to appear in the glass; and when the water sinks below the water-way, the steam will keep what water is in the glass there until the lead plug goes; and then, the driver seeing water in the glass at the time, sticks to his view, and the master, finding the crown of the fire-box down, reasonably concludes that the driver is telling an untruth; whilst the driver reasonably concludes he is hardly dealt with for being discharged. That the fault is due to his negligence cannot be denied, but it is unsatisfactory when the facts are against the evidence, and there is no getting at the truth.

Water in the gauge-glass may really signify absolutely nothing, unless the top water-way is perfectly clear, and hydrostatic equilibrium can be established in the gauge-glass. Much confusion and many lengthened inquiries have taken place through lead plugs blowing out, when, afterwards, the boiler was found to contain plenty of water. Much time would be saved were there two plugs in the fire-box, as practised by Mr. Sturrock. We have duplicate gauge-glasses, which is an admirable arrangement; and why not have duplicate fire-plugs?

The infliction of a fine for not examining an engine before leaving the shed is common; but there is one way of getting over it, as long as a man is upon a railway, and that is to make it a matter of conscience never to turn a wheel without examination. There is not much to do. There is no danger of the boiler tumbling off the frame, or the smoke-box leaving the boiler, or the crank-axle turning end forward. The examination may be all done in fifteen minutes, and if an engine is habitually and daily examined, it can be overhauled in less time; but supposing it takes fifteen minutes to look into the ash-pan, and to see that all the pins and cotters are fast, and all the glands are fair and square with their respective rods, it is a very small matter compared with the answering of a report about a gland coming off, or the fire-bars melting with an ash-pan full of ashes, or a split-pin in the motion being lost, and delaying the train, inconveniencing a number of passengers. Not that engines may not break down, even after having been examined; but if they do, it is a source of satisfaction to know that the failure could not have been foreseen.

We have endeavoured in this chapter to point out the ways in which it is possible to go wrong, and also endeavoured to show how it is possible to go right—or rather, to try and go right; and, in conclusion, we shall show how it is possible to make an incredible mistake.

The driver of a goods-train brought his engine and train to the foot of a home-signal which was against him. He and his fireman had some difficulty in stopping at it; so the engine was reversed, and they sat down, and it is thought that they both went to sleep. The driver happened to open his eyes and saw the signal off, and put on steam. The guard in the rear finding that the train was going the wrong way, and gaining speed, and fearing some one would run into his van, jumped out and showed a red light, of which no notice was taken until the engine came up to him, when he saw that both men were standing facing the weather-board, and quite unconscious that they were going the wrong way.

The driver and fireman of an engine ran a distance of six miles on the wrong road, and crossed over into the other road, and had no sooner done so than an express went by them, which made their hair stand on end to think what a marvellous escape they had had.

THE ACCIDENT NEAR BECKENHAM, ON THE LONDON, CHATHAM AND DOVER RAILWAY.

CHAPTER VI.

RUNAWAY TRAINS.

THE iron monarch is attached to the train, and the platform is full of people, high and low. The bell is ringing to remind travellers that is is just five minutes to departure time.

Everything is ready:—

> " The steam is up; the engine bright as gold;
> The fire-king echoes back the guard's shrill cry,
> The roaring vapour shrieks out fierce and bold
> A moment—and like lightning on we fly."

There is joy in many faces amongst the passengers, and some traces of sorrow in others. Luxury and comfort await some, whilst to others, home is no home; but, whoever the passengers may be, all run at the same speed, and "the shepherd's crook is laid beside the sceptre," for the drivers are devoted to one object, and one only, and that is to carry them all to their destinations. To do this—and it is done with rare exceptions—the man in charge of the fire-king has to keep a vigilant eye upon his charge, and upon the traffic, and to maintain his self-possession. The work performed by our railway engine-men is well done. Sometimes it is performed under exceptional and trying circumstances, arising from the neglect of another, or from occurrences over which they have no control.

The express from the north was coming down a very long incline. As the driver came over the summit, he shut off steam earlier than usual, because it was a heavy train and would require more brake-power to keep it from attaining excessive speed. The brake was put on just to rub the wheels; but, the train gaining speed, the driver intimated with his hand that he required the brake on "harder." This was done by the obedient fireman. Still the speed gained. The driver took to the brake, but it was on hard, so he whistled for the guard to put his brake on hard—a signal which the guard understood, for which the driver makes sharp distinct whistles. Still the train gained speed. It is daylight, and the driver is satisfied that the guard is not asleep; he can see his head out of the window. Still she gains speed, and comes down the incline and round the sharp curves at a mad pace. The driver has put his engine out of gear; he has reversed her; but it is of no avail. At a distance of five miles ahead he is supposed to pull up at a passing station; for the line is single, and there he is timed to pass the south mail. To overshoot that platform may mean the wreck of both trains, as the mail may be just drawing into the platform at the same time as the north express, in ordinary conditions. The driver of the express knew that, and seeing it was hopeless to even dream of stopping at the station, he applied his whistle vigorously. The station-master heard the sharp, distinct, shrill sounds up amongst the rocks. By a kind of divination he interpreted the cause. As quick as thought, this agent jumped upon the

back of a gentleman's horse outside the station, and in a snap
he was off at a gallop through the little goods-yard, up the
line for life and death, for the south mail had been announced
from the next signal-station. The beast was urged along the
six-foot, and the railway-man soon covered some level road for
the north engine-man to pull up on. Amongst the hills, the
steam from the south mail could be seen as a white cloud
rising over the tops of the trees, and she was now right on the
straight. The station-master and his horse attracted the
driver's attention, and he instantly shut off steam, and passed
him. The two engine-men stopped their trains without the
engines touching each other. An accident was averted, and
that by the station-master being a railway-man to the back-
bone. All is well that ends well; but this affair nearly ended
badly, and through what? Fish. Yes; fish. A goods-train
had been up the bank before the passenger-train came down,
which contained putrified fish, the oil from which had run
through the crevices in the floors of the waggons, and down
the axle-irons and axle-boxes, upon the metals. Thus was
annulled the frictional resistance on which the driver relied to
hold the train down the incline. If the train had been fitted
with continuous brakes, the margin of frictional power would
have been sufficient, no doubt, to have held the train. But
continuous brakes were not so much appreciated then as they
are now.

Independent of exceptional cases like the above, some
scores of accidents have happened by trains not having
been under the control of the drivers. Engines have dashed
into terminal stations and have jumped over the stop-buffer,
whilst the engine-man was turning a somersault on the platform. The worst cases have occurred with goods-trains. At
Dover something of this kind can be remembered, as well as at
many other terminal stations.

Now, one source of the mischief is the allowing of the
brake-screw to wear out before it is renewed; and as the
driver seldom handles the brake—for it is not his duty—he
sometimes forgets to make it his duty to examine it until it

CLEARING THE TRACK AFTER THE DISASTER AT ABBOTTS RIPTON.

leads to his having to pay for a new set of stop-buffers, new engine buffer-plank, and compensation to passengers. The chances are that the firm—directors—are not an illiberal lot, and they give him, after having been suspended for a time, another chance to act on the impression that his buffer-beam is as glass, and that his brake-screw as precious as gold, and requires a vigilant eye upon it.

Another cause of overshooting the platform is the dependence of the driver upon the guard doing his share of the braking. This may be assumed at a roadside station, without incurring any risk to the passengers; but unlimited risk is incurred by trusting to the guard when the train is running into a terminus. Some of them have been seen to enter a terminal station sitting down to read the daily paper. A driver cannot know what the guard may be doing; and, therefore, in approaching a terminal station, the train should be thoroughly and entirely under his control, so that the engine may be able to stop the train, by signal, at any part of the station. Many accidents have occurred by the driver's assuming that the platform road was clear, whereas another train may have occupied half, and, to his horror, he has struck it.

If a driver is not thoroughly acquainted with a place, it is better to draw in under a little steam than to run in with the fireman looking into the sand-box with one eye and at the stop-buffers with the other. A train once ran away under very peculiar circumstances, illustrating the necessity for the guards being good railway-men. The driver of the train had gone nutting in a wood. He had obtained leave from the station-master, as the train would not be required for several hours; but before the driver returned it was required at the platform, and a guard went to the goods-yard for it. On the engine-foot-plate the fireman was asleep, and, by command of the guard, he brought the train to the platform. This was an hour before train-time. The guard dropped asleep in his van next to the engine, and the fireman went to sleep again on the foot-plate. When the guard awoke the train was travelling, and he jumped up, having no recollection of starting the train. He looked at the country about him, and, behold! he found the train was going in the opposite direction to that in which it should have gone. The man looked at the engine, and he could see no one on it. Could it be a dream? But, dream or no dream, he was travelling fast towards an open drawbridge. The jaws of death open to swallow him, he scrambled out of the van on to the step, and from there unto the tender, and shut off the regulator, landing the fireman a kick under the ribs, which shook him on to his pins. He jumped up and said, "Fire! Fire! where is the fire?" evidently dreaming, or the kick had put fire into him. The fireman and guard alone were with the train, and it is supposed the fireman must have moved the regulator in his sleep.

But, extraordinary as such incidents may appear, there are many others which surpass those which have been related. Not many years ago, passengers who were waiting for a train were surprised to see their train go by their station with both driver and fireman fast asleep on the foot-plate. The train proceeded until the engine was short of breath, and stopped on a bank which was too much for its strength. The guard, who was in the rear of the train, then jumped down from his van, and found the men in the arms of Morpheus. It is not in the power of any teacher to point to any particular kind of accident and preach upon the possibility of preventing it, and state confidently that such and such things have not occurred.

Now we might state that almost all kinds of accidents have happened. This may look like a wild statement. Have not collisions occurred by neglect of the driver? Have they not occurred by neglect of the signalmen? Have not people been killed and then burned? Have not engines with their trains, with full steam on, met at a pace of forty miles an hour? Was not the climax of accidents reached in the Tay Bridge, when engine, train, and passengers disappeared altogether, and not one left to tell the tale?

Trains have been stopped by the birds of the air and the beasts of the field; by the floods and by snow; and there is nothing new on a railway under the sun.

CHAPTER VII.

THE ROYAL TRAIN.

THE genius and worth of George Stephenson are felt throughout the world, not only by the subjects of Great Britain, but by the sovereign of the realm also, for whom, without the aid of the locomotive, life would not be half so enjoyable as it is. Looking back for half a century at the clumsy engine of that period, and then at the magnificent engines that grace the metals of the present day, the progress made in design and in speed, combined with safety, has no parallel in the history of inventions. The stupendous effects which, during so short a period, have resulted from the application of the steam-engine for running vehicles, are striking attestations of the value of the labours of those immortal engineers who stood by it when it was but a forlorn hope.

To an individual who gives us a poem, a picture, a book, or a new pleasure, or discovers a new country, the world shouts, "Live for ever!" Hark! a voice says, "Shakespere shall not die. Michael Angelo shall live. Stephenson shall be immortalized. Faraday is a 'Son of Light.'" All who have wrought at difficulties, brought order out of chaos, music out of discord, cannot analyse or account for the facile inspiration that led them along. All that they know is, that their work was there; and they cared not to look further into the matter.

We owe all the pleasure of quick travelling to a man whom, at one time, engineers, lawyers, and leading members of Parliament were not ashamed to denounce as an idiot, and who blushed not to advise his consignment to Bedlam. Protesting themselves wise, they became fools. What said the *Quarterly Review*, the mouthpiece of philosophy and literature? "Can anything be more palpably ridiculous than the prospect held out of locomotives travelling twice as fast as stage-coaches? We should as soon expect the people of Woolwich to suffer themselves to be fired off upon one of Congreve's ricochet rockets, as trust themselves to the mercy of such a machine going at such a rate. We will back old Father Thames against the Greenwich Railway for any sum. We trust that Parliament will, in all railways it may sanction, limit the speed to eight miles an hour, which is as great as can be ventured on with safety." This was in 1825.

What said *The Times* in 1875, just fifty years after? "Her Majesty Queen Victoria and suite left Windsor Castle for Balmoral last evening at eight o'clock, travelling by way of Bushbury, Carlisle, and the Waverley route, via Edinburgh, where her Majesty partook of breakfast, after which the train proceeded farther north to Perth, and by way of Dee-side to Ballater Station, where the train arrived at twelve o'clock." Now the distance is 600 miles, and deducting 15 minutes at Carlisle, changing engines, and 15 minutes at Edinburgh, and 30 minutes at Perth, the average speed is 40 miles per hour. So much for the opinion of writers who venture to reckon without the probable progress of all things in view. We have not only the speed that wise men thought proper to suggest should be the maximum allowed—eight miles an hour—but we run now-adays at a pace equal to the square of eight miles an hour. And, further, we not only work to the square of eight, but the passengers travel quite as safely at that speed as passengers did in the stage-coaches of which our grandfathers still delight to "crack" about. "Lor, bless you, they were a sort of glory in the country." "Jolly old coachmen, merry and fat, stuffed full of anecdotes. What features they had, and how they put the brandy and water out of sight! And what an odour of fresh hay there was about them! Nothing to equal it now." This is all very natural; this passionate regret is expressed by Byron:—

" There is not a joy the world can give like that it takes away,
   When the glow of early thought declines in feeling's dull decay.
   'Tis not in youth's smooth cheek the blush alone which fades so fast,
   But the tender bloom of heart is gone, ere youth itself is past."

Life on the King's highway has faded out—extinguished like some bright constellation gone for the night.

The iron horse on the iron highway has given us another and better life, which must be charming to many a man, woman, and child, and must promote human happiness, and tend to make life more bearable.

What is human happiness? Human happiness is to shake hands with your truest and best friends as often as you can, to spend your money together, to cut away, if you will, by your-self to scenes where the woodpeckers build.

" Place men," wrote Plato, " where they may breathe the air of congenial friendship, health and beauty, amid fair sights and harmonious sounds, and they will quickly drink in from surround-ing objects sweet and harmonious influences." To carry out the idea of the philosopher, in ever so humble a degree, the railway service of the country offers every inducement to all classes, great or small in number, mighty or plebeian. To meet the demand of people who are constantly migrating in search of change—and we live by change—every precaution is taken to make railway travelling a success and a triumph over the various forms of the subtle decay which dogs the wheels of the rolling stock. Hence it is that we hear the wheel-examiner at the principal stations tapping the wheels to find out if there is a " dog " in it; that is, a flaw or a crack. Diligence is encouraged by the General Manager, who rewards the man with a half-sovereign who finds a " dog ". Every engine and vehicle is examined every day; but when an engine is about to run the Royal Special Train, it is stopped for a day, and is put through a thorough inspection.

When Driver Somerford came off duty one night, he found orders awaiting him to see the foreman the next morning. He knew what that signified. He was going to be asked a number of questions respecting the performance of his engine under steam with a train.

An engine may be all right, so far as working is concerned, and yet she may be a bad steamer for a long distance; and, on the other hand, an engine may be an excellent steamer under all sorts of conditions, and yet be badly managed; or it may be in the hands of a fidgety fogie, who would at every twenty miles during the run exclaim: " I think we shall do it," " I believe we shall! " " Upon my word we shall do it," and so on. Such men have no confidence when called to do a bit of bold enginemanship. In selecting an engine for the Royal Special Train, the driver also is to be considered. It is customary to choose the best engine and the best man. So, early the next morning, Somerford and his foreman were running over to-gether the good and bad qualities of the engine told off for royal service.

The foreman was himself formerly a driver, and therefore a practical man, and could see what was required to be done to insure success. Besides, his advice was eminently practical and attentively listened to. It is a God-send to have a thoroughly practical man for a foreman, for where it is so there is less fining, less discontent, less changing of hands, less breakdowns, and less conceit and make-believe. Fancy a man being made

ARRIVAL OF HER MAJESTY AT CHESTER STATION.

a locomotive foreman who, to all intents and purposes, is a novice in locomotive driving, who cannot give advice but what is secondhand, who is simply an adept at manipulating figures, which he can make prove anything. But with locomotive engines it is a very different business. As soon as an engine and a driver are selected, they both make haste to get into the best of trim. The driver begins to trim the engine, and driver's wife is as busy as two folks to trim Jim up as neat and as clean as a pink to drive the Queen. Jim's wife is all about amongst the neighbours. She calls in at Mrs. Goody's and informs her she is very busy, and can't stop, for Jim is going to run the Queen. She pops into another neighbour's, and just mentions that Jim is at home; which generally brings out the question: " How is that? " " Oh! haven't you heard, Mrs. Smart? Our Jim is going to drive the Queen to-morrow, and he'll keep time, I'll back."

The engine is placed over a convenient pit, near the top of the road, so that the officials can walk down the steps into the pit and examine the engine most minutely. In the first place, the regular cleaner is assisted by the " gang " of cleaners, that is recruits, who are elated not a little with the honour of cleaning her Majesty's engine. The feelings of loyalty work upon them, and the engine soon shines with " elbow-grease." At the same time, or just before, another gang of men, known as washers-out, set to and clean the boiler out, with hose pipes attached to the main and copper washing-out rods. The hose is first placed over the top of the fire-box, next in the chimney-end, and afterwards in each mud-hole or plug-hole in the bottom of the fire-box. After the boiler is thoroughly cleaned, which is known by the colour of the water running out of it, it is thoroughly examined with a spirit-lamp by the foreman of boiler-makers, who testifies as to its fitness to share in the performance of the trip. How minute the inspection is may be gathered from the fact that every bolt and nut is tested which holds the machinery together.

When the foreman inspects the engine he is accompanied by the driver, who gives an answer to any question which may be put him. The answers to these questions enable the foreman, from practical experience, to form an opinion of what is necessary to be done, in order to make success an absolute certainty. " How do the big-ends run, Somerford? " asks the official. " Very well, sir," replies the driver. " The trimmings are not very old, and I have examined them; they work very moderately, and when the siphon-cups are filled up, they will carry the engine a hundred and twenty miles. I am very particular about my trimmings, and it is necessary to change them as often as it is thought needful, because they get made up with gelatinous matter out of the oil, and I have found them in some engines as hard as corks, and just like pieces of india-rubber. But these big-ends of mine have not been hot for over twelve months, and then it was caused by the cranks striking a heap of ballast, which the platelayers had made too high to clear the engine. Some day or other these heaps of ballast will tear down the ash-pan, and it will be found inside a carriage. The engine runs on the whole very cool; the left-hand leading axle was a plague for a little while, but I had it lifted and the bearing reduced, and it is now running very cool. One of the tender axles was inclined to heat; but that was owing to the horn-plate stay being in the wrong place. The tender had been lifted for new brasses, and the stays were mixed up, and the bolt-holes not being quite fair the horn-plates were sprung in; and when the bolts were in their places the box was fast after a few miles' run. I took them all off one day at Coven, and put them in their proper places. I found they had each a place, and when they were in their own places the axle was free to work, and it has worked satisfactorily since; but before I discovered the cause the tender was a fearful plague. The wheels of the engine have shown no signs of shifting. I had her new out of the shop two years ago, and her wheels have been turned up since. The excentrics have not had the chill off them. I put plug-trimmings in them, like those in the big-ends and outside-rods, and they work very regularly and coolly. The pistons are steam-tight, as well as the valves. I have not had a hot slide-bar for a long time; the last was caused by the cranks hitting the ballast and throwing it all over the engine, when she became smothered with grit. She is in first-class order underneath."

INTERIOR OF THE ROYAL RAILWAY CARRIAGE.

Coming outside, in answer to further questions, the driver continued:— "She is a good steamer, and I have no difficulty with her, so long as the tubes are tight. At one time they were a great trouble; but since the tubes have been referruled they have been as tight as a bottle. I have no trouble with the steam. I instruct my fireman in the matter of firing, and I have my instructions carried out to the letter, or he would get pitched off the foot-plate. Some firemen waste more fuel than their heads are worth; but I always make it my duty to train my firemen, and I turn them off sharply if they are too cockish, and think they can strut and crow about my foot-plate.

"When I was a fireman we had no instructions given us, and if the engine began to blow off we used to put down the damper and open the fire-door. Some men never troubled about the damper, as the handle was placed at the front of the fire-box, so that you had to go round the hand-rail outside every time you wanted to alter it. Of course the cold air going in at the fire-hole made the tubes leak sometimes, but we could not be bothered going outside every now and then. Now we have all the handles quite convenient, and it is no trouble, though some drivers do just the same as before. We used to shovel the coals into the fire-box and allow them to roll anywhere. Now it is different; we have an authoritative opinion how to fire and when to fire, and it makes the iron horse go all the better—more pleasantly than formerly. Why, at one time we were always poking the fire, and the fire-irons were never out of the fire-box, and now many a man's fire-irons are his shovel and coal-hammer. I always work with a con-cave fire, and the coal in actual contact with the heating-surface and the principal mass of the coals over the fire-bar bearers and the centre of the fire self-feeding. The action of the blast and the shaking of the engine roll the lumps into the centre, and the grate is quite open and free from dirt. I am never troubled for steam if we get a strong head-wind or side-wind, which chops the air off the ash-pan front. I fire frequently, so as to keep the smoke out of the chimney, and leave it free for the exhaust-steam to escape. Under such circumstances, the exhaust-steam cannot ladle smoke out of the chimney without expending the power which should clear itself of the chimney-top. So, when the wind blows, I do with as little smoke as possible, so that the exhaust shall not be encumbered with additional work after leaving the cylinder.

"We have had the boiler washed out, all the glands seen to, the tubes cleaned, the fire-bars examined, and the lead-plug seen to."—"You think, then, Somerford, you are in good trim to run the 'Queen?'" asked his foreman. "Well, sir, I will try and give her Majesty a good run," replied Somerford. The polished beauty is all ready long before the fire is required to be lighted, while she is the heroine of the hour and the pride of the shed. Imagination is in full-play as the young cleaner and the young fireman gaze upon her. They fancy that in a few hours' time those huge wheels, under the control of Somerford, will be rushing in all their speed and mighty force by towns and sleeping villages, by pleasant homesteads and grand old churches, and on through hills and valleys, across rapid streams and swamps, out on to the level moors, and away, hidden in darkness, towards dear old Scotland.

This fiery courser has all the marks of " go " about her, and young hearts and young life can already hear her pounding through space and roaring over the rails.

At the appointed hour she is in steam, and stands foaming upon the iron track, impatient to be hitched on to the special. As soon as Her Majesty has arrived at the station, a very few minutes intervene before she gives the order to start, in the midst of the fullest excitement; for wherever the Queen goes, all is bustle and striving to see her face. English people like their Queen, and so the departure platform is always crowded whenever she is going away. A few clear, sonorous puffs, and the huge creature begins to stretch its sinews of brass and muscles of iron, saluting the weary cars in the sidings as it begins to feel the pressure of the load. When a driver has combined his knowledge of the signals and their position with his knowledge of the road and its gradients, he can then run with confidence, without the least fear of losing control over the train. With the special, there is, besides an inspector and a locomotive superintendent, a timekeeper who records the exact times at which the train passes stations. This man and the driver hold short but frequent intercourse, which enables the driver to regulate the speed, and to take the train by the stations just as it is due; and besides, it assists him to keep the proper distance between the pilot-engine and the train. The pilot-engine is run before the royal engine, and it is supposed to have passed each station fifteen minutes before the special. After the pilot has passed, no engine or vehicle whatever must go over the same metals until the wheels of the royal engine and train have run over them. No shunting of carriages or waggons is allowed after the pilot has passed. The fifteen minutes is the Queen's. There is also a printed order issued to every station-master, signalman, and platelayer along the line of route, showing what time the special is expected to pass them in the respective districts, and, moreover, a circular is issued to all those drivers and firemen whose trains are to be on the route, informing them where to put in and shunt for the royal. Every one is deeply anxious to keep clear of this important train. Should any one by accident check or stop it, the poor wretch is soon deluged with letters, asking the reason why he came to make such a blunder. The greatest possible care is taken to insure success; and the royal is always travelling under the eye of the general manager, who is always in the train. As it passes along, the station-master and his staff are out upon the platform some time before she is due, to inspect all the crossing-gates in his district, and to appoint some one to watch that gate with all attention. The siding-points are spiked, so that any evil-disposed person or thoughtless servant could not possibly thwart the intention of the directors to run her Majesty under circumstances all tending to secure safety. A very select number of individuals who live in the neighbourhood of the stations are sometimes allowed to see the train pass. That is all they can see. The speed of the train renders it impossible to distinguish the Queen from another lady. All the provisions for security are worked out in the chief office days before the train is to go, and in the presence of those who are appointed to travel with the train. There must be no deviation from the appointed programme. The engine, bright as gold, in the hands of a skilful engineer soon settles down to her work, and, like lightning, on she speeds with the long trail of carriages sweeping round the curves, now full in view, awe-inspiring, now under ground, and now in the deep cutting, and then upon the level. But the good, noble creature is inseparably dependent

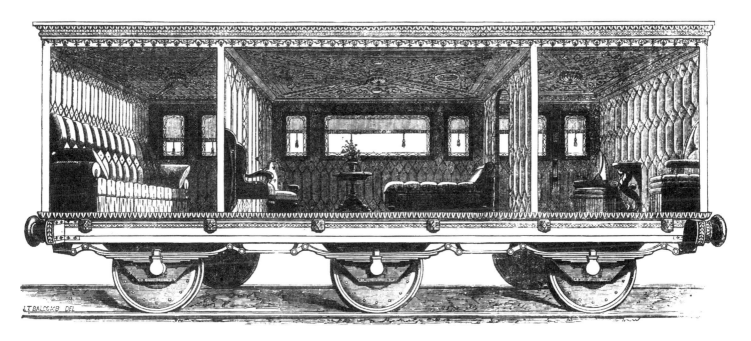

RAILWAY CARRIAGE BUILT FOR THE USE OF THE PRINCE AND PRINCESS OF WALES.

upon the intellect of man which conceived him, and endowed him with strength to drag St. Paul's to Edinburgh if it could be hitched on. Thanks to the achievements of locomotive superintendents, we have at the present time the most magnificent engines in the world, and no one can become the driver of such without fearless toil. On the expresses we see men who have done wonders. From cleaning, at nights as well as day, to firing first on slow goods; from goods to fast meat-trains; from these to slow passenger, and on to the "goers." It is only after long experience that a driver is put in charge of the most important trains in the world. This is how it should be, to obtain the best men for the best service. A driver in charge of a royal train is as much as home as though he

were running an ordinary express. The officials being on the foot-plate might hamper the fireman's movements, but not those of the driver's. He has his position, and there is not a locomotive superintendent in the world who would dictate to him as to his mode of using his engine, because the superintendent selects only such men as work their engines to his satisfaction. Therefore the trip is run under the most pleasant associations.

The Governor-General of Canada and Princess Louise had a narrow escape from a fearful death on the occasion of their recent journey by special train over the North Shore Railway from Ottawa to Quebec. Upon the day fixed for starting, and about ten o'clock in the morning of that day, a special train, comprising a locomotive and three cars, left Hull station, having on board her Royal Highness and the Marquis of Lorne and suite. Calumet, a station fifty-three miles from Ottawa, was to be the first stopping-place. About fifty miles from Ottawa is a small station called Montebello, and it was at this place that the miraculous escape of the Royal party, which we are about to chronicle, occurred. It appears the express train from Montreal to Ottawa was ordered to pass the vice-regal special at Montebello, and was to arrive there first and run in on the switch, in order that the special should not be stopped. The express arrived, ran up the main line beyond the switch, and backed down upon it. They had scarcely backed clear of the switch when the special was heard thundering along toward the station. The trainman, who had opened the switch to let the express back down, tried to close it again, when, to his dismay, he was unable to move it with the lever. He called for help, and no less than four men,

aided with crowbars, were struggling to close it. On came the approaching train, and in a minute a horrible collision must have occurred. Those who saw the situation quailed with fear. Every one felt how utterly helpless they were to assist the men at the switch. The train was approaching at the rate of from thirty-five to forty miles an hour, the engine-man unconscious of the impending danger. At this critical moment a man rushed frantically up the track towards the incoming train, waving his arms wildly about. Without any signal-flag or other thing to indicate his purpose, it was doubtful if his gestures would be understood by the engineer, and if they were, whether the train could be stopped. As soon as the signal was noticed by the special driver, the brakes were applied, and everything done to stop the train; which, happily, was accomplished. but not until the engine had approached within a few yards of the switch. This shows the importance of keeping a good look-out.

CHAPTER VIII.

THE TAY BRIDGE ACCIDENT.

Want does all things:— Builds harbours, roads, canals, aqueducts, and viaducts. It builds lighthouses and breakwaters. It builds the locomotive engines of the present day. No doubt we keep moving onwards, whether we will have it so or not. It cannot be denied that, independent of the names with which each achievement is associated, we are advancing towards an unknown condition of things. But if we analyze all the forms of improvements, we shall find between the lines the traces of anguish and marks of the scorching tear—in a marked degree in the history of iron and engineering. To attribute to iron absolute indestructibility is a fallacy, though nothing is more common than to do so. Its liability to be influenced by variations of temperature, expanding or contracting, is in engineering circles well known; but the treacherousness of iron is awful unless a wide margin of safety is allowed for straining and crushing. One of the most gigantic undertakings of modern times is the bridge over the Tay, constructed in order to secure for the North British Railway Company independent access to Dundee, free from the control of any other company, and free from the inconvenience of a ferry.

In November, 1864, the first plan for a bridge was brought forward, but the design was objected to by the harbour trustees of Dundee, who considered that ships would run against it. Another bridge, at a place lower down, was proposed in 1866. That design fell through for want of cash. In the year 1870, a select committee of the House of Commons sat to inquire into the petition of the North British Railway to construct the Tay Bridge, when the preamble was declared fully proved, and the Bill afterwards came before the House of Lords, where a committee sat, and received evidence of a voluminous character, after which permission to build the bridge, according to the plans exhibited, was given.

The bridge was 3,458 yards in length, and consisted of 85 spans: fifteen of 120 feet; thirteen of 145 feet; thirteen of 245 feet; twelve of 130 feet; twenty-five of 67 feet; one of 170 feet; and six of 27 feet. There were used in its construction, 3,600 tons of wrought-iron, 2,600 tons of cast-iron, 35,000 cubic yards of brick-work, and 87,845 cubic feet of timber. In the middle of the river, the thirteen spans of 245 feet wide, were about 100 feet above low-water level, to allow vessels of large size to pass up and down the river. It was of a pier and lattice construction, carrying a single line of rails, having continuous check-rails throughout. The nearest European example of pier-construction similar to the Tay Bridge, is the Cere Viaduct, in France. It is a single-line viaduct, having piers in clustered column about 100 feet high, and 30 feet wide at the base.

The natural difficulties opposed to the construction of the undertaking at Dundee excited very great interest; and the fame of the noble example of man's skill and ingenuity went far and wide. It was visited by engineers from America, France, and Germany. Some went home and wrote about it; others thought more and said nothing. But, as a bridge, it eclipsed the magnificent structures over the Tamar, at Saltash, as well as the astonishing bridge over the Hollandsche Diep. It was opened in 1878, after having been tested with a downward pressure by running six heavy goods-engines over it to and fro. Of course the side or lateral pressure required to blow it over was a matter of calculation, and was stated to be 96 lbs. pressure per square foot, with a train upon it.

The summer passed, and the autumn died, and December raved for a death-roll. It made one in a hurricane of snow at Abbots Ripton; it had another in a gripping frost at Oxford, and the rapid fall of the barometer indicated mischief brewing in the Tay. The waves were crested with foam, the night was wild, the windows of the houses chattered again, whilst the fury of the swirly gale increased in depth and strength. The Edinburgh driver drew up at the south-end cabin, and received the baton from the signalman, proving to him that the line was clear; and it was not for him to ask more, it was his to obey, and cross with the living freight in that terrible night. Neither he nor his fireman was timorous. They pulled gently away from the cabin, and entered into the raging jaws of the storm. As they advanced it seemed as if the elements were let loose and battling together in fearful antagonism. The wheels and axles groaned against the rails, and flashing sparks shot out from amongst them, as the engine strained every nerve to cross the bridge. The ruthless, wild blast was fiercely sweeping clean across their track; the roar increased, and flash followed flash. The wind in its mad career swept down the Tay from the flat plain of the Carse of Gowrie, and the bridge of Earn.

The bridge repelled the gale until the unfortunate train entered the high girders, 100 feet above the waters; when the furious blast, as though eager for a banquet of slaughter, put forth all its strength, and at one fell swoop hurled girders and train, and living freight, as one mass into the sea. No pen can adequately describe the terrible fall of iron, of steel, of fire, of hissing steam, and of the unfortunate victims. Short as the agony of Mitchell and Marshall may have been, there was a portion of time in which they would realise their dreadful situation more than any person in the train.

When one considers the stupendous character of the gap that was made (1,000 yards), the enormous height of the bridge, and the amount of metal that fell, together with a monster engine and tender, and a complete train with sixty passengers, one can form some idea of the tremendous accident, and one can also conceive what a night it must have been for the roar of the wind to have hushed all in a watery grave, without a single being on shore hearing anything of it. And so the bridge on which we all looked with pride, and had come to regard as a part of the great thoroughfare of this great community, was swept away under the tremendous side-pressure of wind. The train came into the central part when the pressure was scarcely sufficient to blow the bridge over; the train caught the wind still more, when the bridge capsized. After the train left the south end, the signalman telegraphed to the north end by a bell-signal to indicate that the train was on the bridge; after which he made an entry of the fact in a book kept for that purpose. By the side of the cabin-door stood a plate-layer watching the train across the bridge, when suddenly he saw a great flash of fire and the tail-lights disappear. At first the signalman thought that the lights disappeared round the curve in the bridge, and he watched to see if they would come into view again when descending the incline at the north end. As they did not come in view, the signalman tried to ring the signal-bell in the north-end cabin, but he could get no answer. He tried the speaking instruments, and found the communication severed. He and the platelayer were astounded; but after they had collected themselves they walked along the bridge a "wee bit," but the night was so rough that they retraced their steps. "The wind was whistling." They went down to the shore on the east side, and below the bridge; it was dark, and nothing could be heard but the ruthless wind. They went east and went west, but they discovered nothing. The moon was flitting about behind clouds, and ultimately she gave them a glimpse of the awful gap, and then withdrew behind a frowning cloud. They had seen the truth. They were struck with the majesty of the catastrophe, and went to Newport and told the people there what they had seen. The consternation and awe spread from house to house like wild-fire. The signalman in the north-end cabin, when he came on duty for the night, found the weather "blowy." It gradually increased to a hurricane, shaking his caboose, and carrying away chimney cans. He could hear nothing outside but the howling wind, when he received the signal from the south cabin that the train was on the bridge, and in a few minutes afterwards he expected it to pass his box, for which purpose he kept the line clear. He had waited nine minutes, when he began to wonder at its non-appearance. He then went to the top of the cabin stairs, or landing, and looked south for it, and could see nothing of it. All this time the wind was blowing in gusts. He tried to speak with the south signalman on the instruments, and also by bell; but, receiving no answer, he became dreadfully anxious, and went on to the cabin landing again. He could not see anything but the elements battling together. At that moment he was informed by some people who were walking along the esplanade that the bridge had gone. He left the cabin, full of fear and apprehension, and communicated what he had heard to the locomotive foreman, Mr. James Roberts, who was hard by in the engine-shed assisting his men to barricade and secure the doors. He and Mr. Smith, the station-master, made up their minds to go along the bridge in search of the train, notwithstanding the personal risk, for their great anxiety urged them along to see and know, as responsible officers of the railway company, the full extent of what turned out to be a great and unprecedented accident. It was dark, the moon being shaded now and again. As they proceeded they saw a red light on the south side, and at first they had hopes of the train being safe, for they could not realise

VIEW OF THE BROKEN BRIDGE FROM THE NORTH END.

THE TAY BRIDGE ACCIDENT: DIVING OPERATIONS IN SEARCH OF THE WRECK OF THE TRAIN.

the fact that such a dreadful accident was possible as for the whole train to have fallen into the river. They thought the communication had been broken through some telegraph poles having been blown down. But what must Mr. Roberts have thought and felt when he found himself suddenly on the very edge of the gap, and saw the water rushing out of the service-pipe and falling 100 feet down into the boiling waters below, which were then heaving and tossing over the dead, for whom no hearts were yet stricken? There was no noise distinguishable from the roar of the tempest to tell him what the wild waves held; neither did he suspect, with the light shining ahead, that the whole train with its living burden of passengers were engulphed in the billowy flood beneath his feet. Being satisfied as to the fate of the bridge, from the line he went on board a steamer, and saw from the river the full extent of the gap above, after which the notion of the train being on the south side vanished for ever. There was not a single thing to be seen to prove that the train was in the river; but all doubt was by this time dispelled, because they had had information of its leaving the south box, and abundance of evidence to prove that something of an unusual nature had occurred accompanied by continuous flashes of fire. An eye-witness stated at the inquiry that he came out of his house about seven o'clock to see the storm and its effects. The wind at the time was blowing the water into foam, the river was running very high, and the spray was dashing over the north end of the bridge. When within three hundred yards of it, he stood and looked towards it with the view of observing how the structure stood the storm. Almost instantly, he saw a mass of fire fall from the bridge into the river on the east side. The moon was shining out at the time, and was occasionally obscured by clouds, whilst the wind was severe. When he saw the mass of fire fall, he exclaimed to a friend who was with him, ''There's the train in the river.'' He looked to the river to see if he could see anything, and he thought he saw steam or spray rise near the north end of the big pillars. There was nothing to be heard when the body of fire fell, but the howling tempest. He was alarmed, and climbed over the fence of the Caledonian Railway, and shouted to the North British signalman; but what with the wind and the water, he had some difficulty in gaining his attention. Having succeeded, he asked him if the Edinburgh train was on the bridge, and the signalman replied "The Edinburgh train has been signalled ten to fifteen minutes." Then, answered the observer, "I think the train is in the river." Whereupon Mr. Roberts was informed of the matter.

We have endeavoured to give a succinct account of this catastrophe, which is destined, as long as railways exist, to hold an unenviable place in the history of railway accidents;

for, properly speaking, no eye saw it and no ear heard it, and no one survived to tell anything about it; and of sixty-seven persons who went down on that fatal night, the bodies of only forty-five have been recovered.

The engine, No. 224, was a bogey engine—an engine of which the forepart is supported on a carriage running on four wheels, for the purpose of facilitating the motion of the engine on curves, and making a smooth-running engine. The driving wheels were 6 feet 6 inches in diameter, and coupled; the cyclinders were 17 inches in diameter, with a stroke of 24 inches. It was built by the railway company in 1871, at Cowlairs workshops, and was fitted with a Westinghouse brake and two

hand-brakes. The weight of the engine was 34 tons, and the tender, with fuel and water, weighed 24 tons.

In the sad fate of Driver Mitchell and Fireman Marshall we have a graphic illustration of the contingencies of locomotive driving. These men left their homes on the morning of December 28, 1879, never to return again. We find that they managed their engine in every way satisfactorily; and they never felt themselves more capable of conducting their work as well as they did when they set out on this fatal trip.

Before they reached the bridge they had experience of the gale, and it formed a portion of the last conversation which the fireman had with his father a few stations before reaching the Tay Bridge.

Marshall's father came to the station to see his son, and something prompted him to ask them if they were not afraid to be out in such a dreadful night, but they both replied that was nothing when they were used to it. They spoke from experience, and no doubt they had felt before as much wind blowing; and so far as their engine was concerned, they knew they could pull through it, but there their responsibility began and ended. They had no voice nor control over the bridge. It had been erected by eminent engineers of the day, to extend the interests of the railway company by whom they were employed; and, therefore, they would be the last of men to hesitate in crossing it at any time. It was their duty to judge when their engine was not safe, and they would confide in the like quality being possessed by those whose duty it was to say "nay" to crossing the bridge. When we hear of men losing their lives by neglect of their own, we feel that an error has been made which cannot be redeemed; but when men lose their lives in the execution of their duty, we feel how strangely contradictory are human judgments; and the outcome is commiserative feelings for those who laid down their lives for *us*—teaching us that our calculations were wrong, to show us the flaws in the links of our scientific knowledge.

From the Queen down to the humblest of her subjects all

felt sorrowful when they heard that a train had left Edinburgh for Dundee, and that on Tay Bridge a tragedy occurred such as never had taken place in this country. There was lamentation, and mourning, and woe. "Please, sir," said an inquirer, to a person coming from the direction of the station, "can you inform me if the Edinburgh train has arrived?"—"The Edinburgh train, madam, is in the river," replied the man. The fluttering, anxious heart of Mrs. Mitchell gave way, for she had been watching for her husband's return, and she became unconscious. Before any one knew positively that the train was lost, she became anxious, and was therefore making inquiries of passers-by.

Driver Mitchell commenced cleaning engines early in 1864, was made a fireman in 1865, and was promoted to the position of a driver in 1871. So, he had been driving eight years. He was thirty-eight years of age. Mrs. Mitchell was left to mourn his loss with five children, of whom the eldest was under eight.

Fireman Marshall commenced cleaning in 1875, and was made a fireman in the end of the following year. So he had been firing three years. He was not married.

As some persons may be interested to know how the engine and tender were lifted from the bed of the river, it may be stated that the "Henry" was fitted up with horns over the bows, and with strong tackle. After the chains had been made fast below, by divers, they were gradually raised to the surface by means of winches worked by small engines. In connection with the "Henry" there is a little history which shows that the chequered story of accidents is not confined to bridges or railways. The "Henry," built and belonging to Shields, was wrecked on the Island of Lewis some 45 years ago when she was seven years old. Mr. Birnie bought and raised the wreck, and brought her to Montrose, where she was fitted up, and ran between Montrose and Quebec for many years. She afterwards served in the Baltic and the Quebec timber trade.

CHAPTER IX.

LAST TRIPS.

WHATEVER has been done to make railway travelling safer has conduced to the comfort and safety of engine-drivers. But, notwithstanding such facts, we find in engine-driving life many chapters of melancholy catastrophes, tales of matchless danger, and instances of sharp but sudden sacrifices of life.

There are not more than two or three accidents exactly alike in all particulars; which is an assurance that no accidents happen but the officials put in action counteracting means to prevent their being repeated. Still we find some new foe dogging the wheels of our trains, never satisfied without a funeral pile.

Truly we pay for our railway experience with life, dear life. There is scarcely an improvement which has not been brought about by suffering and death; and the dreadful thirst for victims is as keen as ever. Not all the combined wisdom and sagacity of scientific men can grapple with the Hydra-headed victor. Cut down and disarmed to-day in the east, it springs up again in the west, and new victims fall, never to rise. Art, with all its life-saving apparatus and its plans of improvements, is engaged upon the accomplishment of the great work of emancipating our engine-men from accidents; still these happen.

Every accident that occurs is investigated with minuteness, and the circumstances are recorded with painstaking care, by trained experts and writers. Still they happen. Plans with-out regard to expense or labour are prepared for the inquiry. Officials of the Board of Trade, with ability of the most ponderous description, investigate every case. Still they happen. Government, with public interests and life, precious life, to support it, grapples resolutely with cases, and the truth is shaken out in a manner which could only be done by professors in the art of sifting truth from falsehood—golden grain from subtle chaff. Still they happen. Patient and indifferent to time, the task assigned the inspectors is performed in integrity of purpose and intensity of earnestness to a degree which proclaims each investigation as perfect and as efficiently performed as human ingenuity can make it. And still, from the nature of machinery and from human fallibility, they happen.

A driver and fireman may get through the first and second stages of a trip, or may have travelled for thousands of miles, and yet drivers and firemen are often plunged into eternity without notice. Force to force opposed, the engine is hurled from the track over the embankment, burying him who a moment before held the regulator in the pride of manhood and health. Not all the gigantic brains, energy, and iron will of individuals can contend against natural laws.

Are we perfect? No. What are the facts? Boiler-work has advanced to such a degree that an explosion is of very rare occurrence. Have not wheel-fastening and wheel-making received incessant attention? Has not the whole system of signalling been improved by "blocking" and by fixing signals where engine-men can see them early, and not, as formerly, planted so obscurely as to compel men to strain their eyes out to see them? Look at the block system, which controls the railways, and affords the means of working a heavy and quick passenger traffic. Still, mishaps follow the wheels like bloodhounds, and accidents, to which men, with innate foresight and acquired skill can, by incalculable knowledge in their heads, contribute nothing, not an atom, until the victim is slain, a grief to all, a triumph to the foe. We shall briefly follow one through his career—as good an engine-man as ever took charge.

From tending "nibbling sheep," and reposing on a bed of blossoming health, he obtained a berth in the running-shed. He was the only child of his mother, and she a widow. After he had obtained a doctor's certificate certifying that his health was good, he entered the railway service as a cleaner. He possessed an inquiring spirit, and gave no little attention to all questions connected with the locomotive. His education had been curtailed by the cruel hand of fate. Toil cast its sombre shadow over his young heart ere it had felt the sunshine of a dozen summers, but he broke his bread with simplicity, and pulled hard with his mother through the cold winters, in wind and in rain, amid many vicissitudes. His stock of books was very limited—"Robinson Crusoe," "Belisarius," "The Wide Wide World," "Life of Wellington," "Young's Night Thoughts"—from these he wrested their meaning. He knew nothing of grammar until he accidentally picked up a copy of "Cobbett's Grammar" at a fair, from a book-stall where the owner was clearing out, and refusing no reasonable price. That book was a precious treasure, and he chewed its contents until he knew what savoury was required to make a palatable literary pastry. He sold a couple of rabbits, and walked twenty miles to buy a second-hand Johnson's dictionary, which cost every penny he had in the world; but he was happier than a king. His library was contracted, to be sure, so were his means; but he knew that as he grew older his means would improve and his book-shelves look fatter; so towards manhood he grew, gentle, pure, honest, and brave.

He went through all the hardships of a cleaner's life, drank his warmed-up tea in the furnace-hole, and without a murmur partook of what He who feeds sparrows had given him.

After passing through the grade of a fireman, first on goods, and then on passenger-trains, he became an engine-man; and but few men took possession of the regulator having such a fund of locomotive experience. He let nothing slip—not a bit: if there was a cylinder-cover off, he would seize the opportunity of examining the cylinder; if a dome-joint was broken, he would look into the boiler with a keen relish; if the safety-valves were out, he would examine them, and find out the meaning of flat-face and mitre valves. He would assist in putting together a big-end, in making a trimming, in lifting an engine, in taking down the excentric-rods to lengthen them or shorten them, as the case might be; and, when the fitter was setting valves, he would assist to pinch the engine for him. In a word, he worked his brains as well as his muscles. Whosoever you are that have wits enough to discover the philosophy of such a spirit of inquiry, go and do likewise. Without such attention no man can become a locomotive engine-man of repute. There was another good feature in his character rarely to be met with, and that was, he was never plagued with an overwhelming sense of self. He knew nothing of the ignorance and prejudices that led others to roll themselves up in conceited notions, which is as grave a fallacy as the one entertained by the ostrich, which hides its head in a bush and thinks its whole body is secure. As for our engineer, all the mysterious demonstrations of locomotive science he had examined, and he was simple-hearted enough to think and believe *all* other engine-men were likewise in full cry; and that whatever he had hunted down and unearthed and obtained the mastery of, it was *there* for others to enjoy, not for a day, but for a life. Men knew this. They could approach him; and to the younger hands he was a giant that removed obstacles which they found in the study of steam and steam-engines; and the liberality with which he spared his own for their sake made him, in their eyes, intellectually a head and shoulders higher than his mate. He never turned a lad away without feasting him with bits of good engineering.

"A breath of encouragement sends round the mill;
A breeze of disparagement makes it stand still."

He was always the same. As an engine-man he had no equal; he had a master-passion for the iron steed, and nothing ever happened to him but of which he could divine the cause, as it were, by instinct. It is idle to deny this gift. Some men cannot grasp a locomotive difficulty instantly, and shake the truth out of it, without a deal of pressure being brought to bear upon them; whilst there are men who with half an eye can see at a glance the complaint. In a word, some men will actually deem a strain or a breakdown unassignable; another will diagnose the complaint and prescribe the remedy. Such insight can only be acquired by painful labour and hard-earned experience, supported by the love of the subject. By close observation, either on the foot-plate or on the framing, by constantly listening to the *sound* of the beat, the ear is trained, as in music, to detect the slightest discord or irregularity. But it is evident that a man, if he wishes to become a *master workman,* must study diligently to be *always* prepared to act with precision in an emergency. Having broken down, the first thing we ask is, "What is it?" Many an engine-man has been in a fog to try and find an answer to that question with a reasonable degree of readiness.

When the engine-man took possession of his engine, he little thought how soon his position of responsibility would cease. His success was all due to one thing—he neglected nothing. And it was this cardinal point which all along had helped him to climb the ladder of promotion, and in many instances to leave many of his mates behind who had started cleaning when he did. One day, a visitor at Michael Angelo's studio remarked to the great artist, who had been describing certain finishing touches to a statue, "But those are only trifles." "It

may be so, *in your opinion,*" replied the sculptor, "but recollect that trifles make perfection, and perfection is no trifle." In this exalted spirit the fated driver examined his engine for the fatal trip before he joined his train. He inspected it thoroughly and systematically, having been convinced from experience that it was the only way to obtain and maintain his sovereignty over it. It is a very uncomfortable feeling to be working an engine which one fears may give out every minute; and unless it is properly examined, how can a driver know but that, before he has finished his day's work, the glands may come off, or a big-end cotter work out through a set-screw not being properly pinched up. Such things have taken place, and simply await like conditions to occur again.

When the engine is properly examined, the driver derives from the practice a wonderful amount of confidence in his engine. Without this confidence, a driver is perpetually on thorns, and the least thing out of the common leads him to illusions. Habitual examination leads a man home as safe as he was when he left it, unless some one else blunders over whom he has no control. When our departed engine-man left the shed, he never felt more sure of conducting his engine home again without an accident. Everything was in the best working order.

With the gauge-lamp the engineer examined his own side of his engine, from the trailing-axle of the tender to the leading-axle of the engine, and then underneath, where he scrutinised minutely the crank-axle, with its excentrics and big-ends. Every pin, and cotter, and trimming came under review: with the siphon-taps on the big-ends, which in some engines do occasionally slack back and lose the oil. The corks and buttons were also examined, and were found in good working order, and all the cups filled with oil. This work is done by the fireman, who must have a beginning, and learn to oil before taking charge of an engine. The motion was properly examined, and the glands left fair with their respective rods. The damper was lifted, and a proper examination made of the ash-pan and the lower side of the grate-bars. Coming again outside, the smokebox door was overhauled, and then the fireman's side of

THE ACCIDENT TO THE FLYING DUTCHMAN: RESCUING PASSENGERS.

the engine, together with the tender-coupling and feed-bags, which concluded a minute but an absolutely essential examination. After oiling the tail trimmings a little, preferring to fill the siphon-cups up when in the siding waiting for the train, he left the shed.

Unnumbered—not counted here—are the brave engine-men and brave firemen who have left their homes never to enter them again—hurled headlong, at a moment's notice, into the presence of God. There are William Wolstonecroft, Thomas Taylor, John Horton, Anthony Sharr, Tom Pepper, John Cartwright, Moses Oldknow, Owen Roberts, express men, as brave and as faithful to duty as ever broke bread; who handled the regulator from shire to city on engines the very pride and pick of the road; men that knew no fear, and who never flinched in the fury of speed surrounded by darkness and thunder. They sleep a sleep that knows no waking. Drivers, all of them, thoroughly acquainted with locomotive working and railway traps; men that one would think would be the last to get picked up.

Taylor, the woods ringing with the anthem of song from a thousand throats, was turned by the hand of an erring signalman into a river, and he and his fireman were not divided in death.

In Wolstonecroft were combined the accomplishments of a thorough engine-man with an honest, open mien—polite, affable, sprightly, capable of speaking to please; a good husband, a loving father. He was in charge of a fast express, and whilst tired nature's sweet restorer was paying a willing visit to many eyes unsullied by tears, he was looking out for signals in a dense fog; but before he saw the signal he struck right into a goods-train, and his fate marked him for a victim for the improvement of railway working. His mangled body and that of his fireman lay side by the side of their engine, which was on its side.

Golightly persevered for years to surmount all the disadvantages arising from his old parents not having been able to afford him any schooling, and although he was no scholar, he was successful as an engine-man; but the moral of his success lay in his coming on duty plenty of time before train hours. No

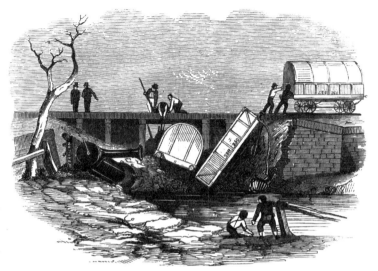

ACCIDENT CAUSED BY COLLAPSE OF A BRIDGE.

one could complain of his engine-manship; it was perfection, and it was only in trifles that he excelled. He opened the regulator like other men, and his engine kept time like those of other men; but there was an indescribable charm about the manner in which he did things, such as only can be acquired by engine-men with long practical experience. When Golightly left home, tempests o'er tempests rolled, and the wind blew a terrific gale. He kissed his wife and his four little dears, and walked into the darkness of night. Ah! into the valley of the shadow of death. The northern blast rattled in the chimneys and in the trees, and as they bowed their hoary tops, seemed to relate in murmuring sounds the dark decrees of Golightly's fate. "What of the night, Ambrose?" said the driver to the night-turner—a dear old soul—as he entered the driver's room to see and hear what was footing afresh. "I think it is a nasty night, Joe; the trains are all late, and there is no hurry for you to go out, for the mail is thirty-five minutes late, and it blows 'big guns' north of the Tweed. What sort of a horse is that of yours in a wind?"—"She is very good," replied Golightly; "but not very grand in a head-wind, and not at all sprightly in a side-wind."—" You must," answered the engine-turner, "look after that mate of yours to-night; he must keep a bright fire, Joe, and keep the smoke out of the chimney. It's the smoke that chokes the engine. Keep the smoke down and the steam up, and she will pull through it. If you get the tubes and chimney full of smoke in a gale, it can't leave the chimney-top unless you work very heavy, and that runs away with the coal, Joe. Keep the smoke down, and I'll be bound she will answer the regulator. She is on No. 6 Road, near the top of New England shed; your fireman is here. Good night, Joe."— "Good night, Ambrose," said Golightly, as he closed the cabin-door, and bid adieu for ever. In half an hour after he was in the siding waiting for the mail, and when it came up the north engine hooked off and he hooked on to it. The signal was given "right away," and Golightly dug into it; his engine answered the whip and steamed splendidly; he did not forget the advice of Ambrose, and took particular notice that a little fuel at a time was charged into the fire-box. In fact, he men-mentioned to his fireman the conversation he had had with the turner. It was a tremendously rough night; and therefore, without such advice, the shovel was working between the fire-box and coal in the tender incessantly. "I think," said he to the fireman, "we are pulling up a little time; but, in a night like this, they must be satisfied if we can keep time." Looking at his watch he found he was just keeping time. "A little bit more fire, mate; I think we can do it if the Northern men can't. What do you say if I sing a song to enliven the heart?" asked the driver. "What would you like? one of the Lancashire poet's?"—"I would, Joe," replied the fireman, "for I want something to make the shovel work, for she's burning a lot of coal."—"One more round, mate," said the driver, "then I will give you Bain's 'Manchester Improving Daily.' " The fire-door was swinging to and fro under the direction of the driver's hand, when the engine gave a lurch. His hand was instantly raised towards the regulator, which he tried to grasp,

but he was thrown head first to the fireman's side of the engine, for she was on her way down an embankment. The suddenness of the occurrence deprived both men of any chance of their recovering their hand-hold; they were no sooner pitched into one place than the plunging movements of the de-railed engine sent them flying into another position. Golightly's neck was broken, and the fireman fell into a hedge which broke his fall, and, except a few scratches, was unhurt. The accident was caused by a piece of timber lying in the way of the mail; the timber had fallen off a goods-train. Surely it can be said of our railway engineers, "In the midst of life they are in death."

*   *   *   *   *

Driver Williams ran over a bale of wool, which threw his engine off the rails into a field and he was scalded—literally boiled alive. Driver Horton ran into some trucks that had been blown out of a siding, and some of the débris struck him on the head and dashed his brains out. This was a sad case; it occurred on his birthday, and within eight hours of his having given a daughter away in marriage. Driver Shaw was killed in broad daylight, one summer afternoon, within sight of some reapers who were the cause of his death. Poor Shaw, he died amidst the incense of ripe corn and wild flowers by the side of a rippling brook, and in the arms of strangers. The reapers, to get out of the sun, had betaken themselves to the railway arch. The arch contained straw, but that did not prevent them setting down their kettle and pans there. In the one they make tea from the leaves of dandelions, in the other whatever come first. Not infrequently reapers keep a dog, and the poor doggy works as well as they do, and occasionally finds a rabbit or a hedgehog, and in return they find him in bones and bits of dry bread. But dogs are such faithful and devoted friends to man that they never complain. Through some carelessness the straw under the arch caught fire, and the wood-work of the bridge being dry and full of tar, it soon blazed, to the consternation of the affrighted reapers, who, hearing a train coming, mounted the railway embankment with the object of stopping the train. The driver and fireman saw the reapers making their own kind of signals to stop them, and looking ahead for the object of danger they saw the smoke and flames issuing from the bridge up the sides and in the centre. They knew not how long the bridge had been on fire, in fact they knew not whether there was a bridge left that would support the train. Approaching at a dashing speed when they first saw the reapers, there was not time to pull up. They tried to pull up with the brake-power in their possession, and by reversing the engine, but they found it impossible. So just as they neared the bridge, they saw from the extent of the lapping flames they should be burned, and so they jumped off the engine. The driver had jumped before, about four years back, when he was ruptured; and being a heavy man, as well as being weak inside, when he fell he lay insensible and bled profusely from his mouth and ears. When the reapers ran to him he was dying. The fireman jumped clear of the train and was saved, but such jumps for dear life are more or less attended by injuries, which young hearts with young blood and limbs make light of, though in after years they are forced to doctor themselves for complaints which can be easily traced to the system having been severely shaken.

Driver D. Jones, fresh and vigorous as the spring, was mowed down by a drunken passenger who pulled the communication cord, when Jones instantly shut off steam, and went to look out between the engine and tender. His head came in contact with a bridge column, and he was cast to earth—dust to dust.

Driver Legge was blown up with his boiler. His arms and legs were hurled in different directions, and one of the former actually went through the window of a private house and fell upon a breakfast-table round which the family were sitting at the time.

Driver Morgan was killed through a telegraph-boy's mistake. A goods-train, through being overlooked, came to a stand in the elbow of a curve in a cutting between two block stations on a single road. The driver was unable to move them with the steam blowing off, so he divided them and ran ahead to the station. It happened that a passenger-train was due at the station in the rear of the goods-train, and when the telegraph boy saw the goods-engine and *some* waggons, he jumped at the conclusion that the whole of the train was there, and accordingly signalled the passenger-train on. The goods-driver stopped at some distance from the station to put off trucks, and as he held the block ticket he thought there was no necessity to tell the station master, and so, when he had put all the waggons away, he returned for the others. Before he reached them he saw a cloud of black dust ascend into the air. That was sufficient. The rest is easily told. The passenger-train which the lad had signalled on ran into the remaining portion of the goods-train, which being in a curve prevented Driver Morgan from seeing it in time to avoid a collision. His went right through the guard's van and into a truck on the other side of it. Hence, the engine fell over into the ballast with the driver underneath, and his fireman; and there died one as faithful to duty as any who have died on a field of battle.

Driver Pepper, in charge of a fast express—and who was more fit to have charge?—was steaming north with a magnificent " goer " in a snow-storm. All appeared to be going well, as it had gone with him for years, upon which he had raised a reputation second to none. Suddenly a goods-train appeared ahead, and with a fearful summons he was called upon to act. Extreme danger threatens, the sharp sound of the whistle is heard in the guard's van, and arrests the attention of the neighbouring villagers; the brakes are instantly applied, the the engine is reversed, her machinery is set, and her driving-wheels are skidding. It is hopeless; a collision must occur. Both driver and fireman see the danger to which they are exposed, and they are distracted. They agree to jump from their engine. Pepper leaps off and is seen to roll over and over like a ball. He is dead. The fireman follows; he shares no happier fate. He breathes a moment; his back is broken. He is gone. The perils of locomotive driving are such that in some instances no possible amount of foresight can avail.

A driver may have equipped himself with all possible knowledge respecting engines, signals, and the traffic. A man may have bundles and bundles of notes dealing with every question in every condition, and gathered from all quarters of the service, to serve in instances when the judgment is called upon to act instantly without any confusion, vacillation, or distraction, and yet it shall not avail him in the hour of peril.

or in books. It was an easy task for her to make out a report, detailing the particulars of a collision, giving a full account and not saying one word more than was necessary.

By this means she became acquainted with the whole system of railway working. She had also been accustomed to watch hour after hour for her father, when he was delayed by a breakdown, or by some accidental occurrence, and so she was trained for a driver's companion. Still, she had her fears when Fred was over his time; she knew his steed was one of the fleetest,

THE ABBOTTS RIPTON ACCIDENT: THE SCENE ON THE FOLLOWING MORNING.

Now our friend the engineer whom we left coming off the shed to join his train was another dead man when he left home,— as pretty a crib as any man could wish for, with as loving a wife as falls to the lot of but few men. He had laid his mother in the grave by the side of his father, and had courted Polly Golightly, whose father was killed on their wedding-day. Polly had been reared almost on the foot-plate; she knew by living in an atmosphere of engine-talk what cranks were, and what would cause a big-end to get hot.

Polly was a girl who knew the whole construction of a locomotive, for the house was full of engines, either in pictures

and she knew his hand and eye were steady. But whenever he was late, each footfall within hearing she listened to, and when she heard his it was sweetest melody. "He's home again," she would ejaculate to herself, and rush forward to meet him. Ah! my dear girl, he is gone at last. Fred Knight, after leaving with his train for the south, experienced all the advantages of trained enginemanship, and, in all the ecstasy of motion, the glare of the head-light spread around the head of his engine as usual, and there was nothing to occupy the mind out of the common routine of foot-plate work. The night was dark and frosty, but still it was a pleasant sky, and he was

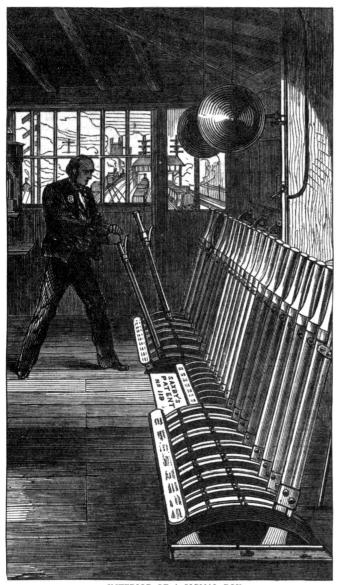

INTERIOR OF A SIGNAL BOX

keeping time. He knew all the working of the traffic thoroughly, and expected to see local or through goods in the sidings where they were timed to shunt for the mail, if he did not pass them shunted before they could reach the appointed siding.

One of these local goods-trains arrived at Holly Bush siding to shunt for Fred, who was in charge of the mail, for which all goods are supposed to leave the main-line fifteen minutes before it is due. When the goods arrived opposite the signal cabin, the driver shouted to the signalman, " I am going into the siding for the mail, and when I am clear of the main-line I'll whistle." " All right," replied the signalman; " be as sharp as you can, for she's due in ten minutes." The goods driver took his train up the line to a siding which was not under the control of the signalman, but worked with drop points. The under-guard held the points, and the head-guard called the driver back with a white light, which signifies, " All right." When the driver began to set back, he found the rails were either very slippery or the brakes were on in the guard's-van. He ascertained that the front brake was off, by sending his fireman to look. He reversed his engine ahead, and reversed into them with very little success, and at last he concluded the rear brake must have been left on, and he *whistled* sharply for it to be taken off—a performance well understood between driver and guard. Considerable time had been occupied before he whistled, but when he did whistle, the signalman had the mail on—he had hold of distant-signal lever, dreading to delay or check the mail for a second—and when the goods driver whistled, he took all the signals off, and Fred came up at a dashing speed, and ran right into the goods, which was half in the siding and half out of it. His engine struck a cattle-waggon first, containing twelve cattle-drovers asleep. These were the first to be killed. Fred's engine, striking with the near buffer, took right across the down road over a bit of embankment, and rolled down the slope to the bottom, amidst showers of sparks and belching steam. As soon as possible the driver of the goods ran to the mail engine, but for some time he could not approach the engine for scalding water and issuing steam; and, what was more sad, he could not find either of the men. After waiting for the steam to clear away, he found Fred, or rather his mortal frame. The vital spark was gone. He could have known neither the bliss nor the pain of dying; he knew nothing either of the sting or victory of death; for his death was instantaneous—caused by a blow on the forehead—supposed to have been caused by the regulator handle, and one thigh was broken, which no doubt was done after he was rendered insensible.

The fireman was crushed to death under the engine. The signals were all right for Fred, and he had not the slightest chance of preventing the accident.

But there was one man who could have prevented it, and who should have prevented it, and that was the under-guard of the goods-train. The signalman stated in his evidence that if the tail-lights of the goods-train had not been changed until the whole of the train was in the siding, he should not have lowered the signals. As it was, the under-guard changed the lamps before he held the points to turn the train into the siding, which was done to save him the trouble of walking the length of the train to change them, after the engine was on the points.

When a goods-train or any other train is on the main-line, it exhibits red lights on its way. Should it go into a siding to shunt for another train, the lamps are turned so as to exhibit white lights; which means to an approaching driver, " It's all right; we're in the siding." To save trouble, and to save his legs, the under-guard changed the lamp from red to white before he was in the siding, and even before he had left the main-line. Such a practice, when followed, should be visited most sharply. Then, again, the signalman was deficient in his practice, because he knew what kind of a whistle indicates " right," and what indicates annoyance. A few sharp whistles means, " Look out, guard; there's something wrong some-where; " and it remains for the experienced guard to interpret such a sound. But, " all right," when safe or clear of a fouling road, has for years been expressed on the steam-whistle by

" crowing." There is no doubt that a considerable degree of security is insured by using a code of whistles. No doubt the whistle will be much improved, so as to emit different tones, each having a definite meaning. For want of a code, with a strict observance of rules, fourteen people lost their lives—driver, fireman, and twelve cattle-dealers—together with twenty head of cattle. None of the passengers were injured, for the engine-tender coupling broke, and none of the carriages left the rails. One of the first-class carriage-doors flew open, and a lady was thrown out, but she was comparatively uninjured. It was decided, after this sacrifice of life, to connect the siding-points with the signalman's box, so that when the points were open to the main-line the signalman could not lower the distant-signal—a system known as interlocking.

It was soon known at head-quarters what had happened, and then commenced one of those most painful tasks of break-ing the sad intelligence to the wife, who most likely had to be called up out of a sound sleep to hear of her loss. It was arranged that a neighbour's wife, whose husband had just come home, should call her, and say there was a rumour that Fred had had a collision. But Polly knew too much of rail-way life not to see there was something behind that. Fred had been in collisions, and she knew that Mrs. Joyce would not come to fill her bosom with fears about that which might simply amount to a few hours' loss of time. With a wild shriek she threw up her arms and exclaimed, " My Fred's dead, Mrs. Joyce! I knew that when I heard the knock at the door. Oh, tell me at once; don't keep me in suspense! Is he suffering, Mrs. Joyce? "—" No, my dear," said she.—" Ah, my Fred, my Fred! thou art gone! " and she swooned away. Intense is grief when it comes suddenly and in the dead of the night; but many a woman wedded to a driver has passed through the ordeal with remarkable firmness and fortitude—because, maybe, they are not strangers to such ordeals. At a locomotive depôt seldom a week passes but some one is either killed or is maimed for the remainder of his life.

Polly's grief was most poignant. She had lost her father,

and had now lost her Fred, who had climbed upwards step by step. They had struggled to make a comfortable home, and now, just when they had surmounted all difficulties, her husband was snatched away in the flower of life. The ways of Providence to man are often very mysterious; but railway men need a special Providence. So many wheels revolving, so much independent action and individual supervision, and so wide a scope for the chances of human fallibility! All was not lost to the world when Fred died. His character remained behind to enrich others as certainly as the rich man's wealth remains behind to increase the estate of his heir. How we watch with interest the swelling of a rose-bud in the spring! How we sigh in sadness when its glory is ruthlessly scattered! But still, when that has happened, we gather the shed leaves from the ground and deposit them in a place of safety, and soon we make the glad discovery that in these leaves, even when withered, we retain for enjoyment the fragrance of the rose both in the winter and in summer, when the living flower, fresh and dewy on its leafy stem, can never be restored.

The following lines are very appropriate to his memory:—

" My engine now is cold and still,
  No water does my boiler fill;
  My coal affords its flames no more,
  My days of usefulness are o'er;
  My wheels deny their noted speed,
  No more my guiding hand they need;
  My whistle, too, has lost its tone,
  Its shrill and thrilling sounds are gone;
  My valves are now thrown open wide,

My flanges will refuse to guide;
  My clacks, also, though once so strong,
  Refuse to aid the busy throng.

No more, I feel each urging breath;
  Life's railways o'er, each station past,
  In death I'm stopped, and rest at last.
  Farewell, dear friends, and cease to weep;
  In Christ I'm safe—in Him I sleep."